SWANSEA

HISTORY YOU CAN SEE

SWANSEA

HISTORY YOU CAN SEE

RICHARD PORCH

TEMPUS

Frontispiece: Wind Street, Swansea in the mid-Victorian period.

First published 2005
Reprinted 2007

Tempus Publishing Limited
Cirencester Road, Chalford
Stroud, Gloucestershire, GL6 8PE
www.tempus-publishing.com

British Library Cataloguing in Publication Data.
A catalogue record for this book is available from the British Library.

ISBN 978 0 7524 3076 8

Typesetting and origination by Tempus Publishing Limited.
Printed in Great Britain.

Contents

	Acknowledgements	6
	Introduction	7
	Bibliography	8
one	A–Z of Swansea's history	9
two	History you can see in a street name	121
	About the author	127

Acknowledgements

Bernice Cardy, Swansea Museum; Sue Hughes, Glamorgan Gwent Archaeological Trust; West Glamorgan Archives for permission to use the pictures of Aberdyberthi Street in the 1930s, the Tennant Canal in the 1930s and the city centre redevelopment drawings done in the 1940s. The Royal Commission on the Ancient and Historical Monuments of Wales for permission to use the aerial image of fish weirs in Swansea Bay; Central Reference Library Swansea; Ken and Elaine Hughes of Trallwn Farm; Dr Ronald Austin and Dr Geraint Owen at Swansea University; the City and County of Swansea for giving me the opportunity to write this book; Gary and Mary Iles of Overton House; Sean Hathaway, Environment Officer for the City and County of Swansea; Phil Keatley for assistance with aspects of the research; Judith Porch for her patience; Edwin Green, Archivist at HSBC Holdings plc; Dr Fiona Wells at the Vincent Street Translation Unit; Mr and Mrs D. Rees for background information on Llansamlet; Mr and Mrs G. Watkins for help with aspects of the history of Trallwn; and the Conservation Section of the Planning Department. I would also like to convey my appreciation to Katherine Burton at Tempus Publishing for her help and guidance in the writing of this book.

Introduction

This does not pretend to be a conventional local history book. By that I mean that it does not proceed in an orderly fashion from earliest beginnings to modern times in anything approaching a chronological fashion. If at any time it appears to, this is purely accidental. The ethos behind the book rests on the understanding that I have tended to write about history on the basis that I have stumbled across it while walking around Swansea. I am very interested in the sort of history that you see every day – yet do not see. I also believe that history can reside as much in a street name as in a familiar old building or a landmark. I've tended to steer clear of the more obvious historic artefacts that come to mind, such as this or that castle or any similar ruin. In fact, the only castle I do write about – Morris Castle – is not actually a castle although it is thought of as such by local people. This book is about more commonplace historic items, the sort you can literally stub your toe on while walking around. That's my sort of history: the hidden history that maybe now resides only in a forgotten nameless lane on a map. What I hope you will discover is that, historically, most things in Swansea seem to interrelate one way or another. You will find that certain names crop up again and again, as do certain organisations, commercial or civic. This is unavoidable and in any case provides a useful connecting thread in the absence of a chronological structure to the book. I make no bones about the choice of subject matter being idiosyncratic; I've tended to write about things as I found them. If I seem to over-visit certain geographic locations at the expense of others, I can only apologise and cite habit rather than favouritism. There is much 'history you can see' all around you. It can be found at a large scale in the geology of the place you live in or at a small scale in the materials used in the construction of a garden wall. The very stones our houses and pavements are made of all have a story to give up and you often don't have to 'dig' too hard to find it.

If nothing else, I hope this book will make you curious about everything you see around you – you only have to look.

Bibliography

Boorman, David, *The Brighton of Wales*, Swansea Little Theatre Company Ltd, 1986.

Griffiths, Ralph A. (ed.), *The City of Swansea – Challenges & Changes*, Alan Sutton.

Gwynn, D.R., P.R. Reynolds and H.K. Warren, *A Postal History of Swansea and District*, Swansea Philatelic Society.

Hayling, Nigel, *A Stone and Wattle Fish Weir Complex in Swansea Bay*, Swansea Bay Intertidal Survey GGAT 58.

Hilton, K.J. (ed.), *The Lower Swansea Valley Project Report*, Longmans, 1967.

Hughes, Stephen and Reynolds, Paul, *The Industrial Archaeology of the Swansea Region*, Association for Industrial Archaeology.

Hughes, Stephen, *Copperopolis*, RCAHMW [Royal Commission on the Ancient and Historical Monuments of Wales].

Lavender, Stephen, *New Land for Old*, Adam Hilger Ltd, Bristol.

Newman, John, *The Buildings of Wales – Glamorgan*, Penguin.

Pierce, Gwynedd O., *Place Names in Glamorgan*, Merton Priory Press, 2002.

Thomas, Norman Lewis, *The Story of Swansea's Districts and Villages*, Vol. II.

Williams, Herbert, *Welsh Stagecoaches*, Barry, 1977.

W.H. Jones, History of the Port of Swansea, Carmarthen, 1922.

Gower Journal, XV, XX, XXIV.

Lower Swansea Valley Factsheets, Swansea Museum.

Minerva, Vol. 1, 1993.

Swansea Before Industry, Swansea Museums Service.

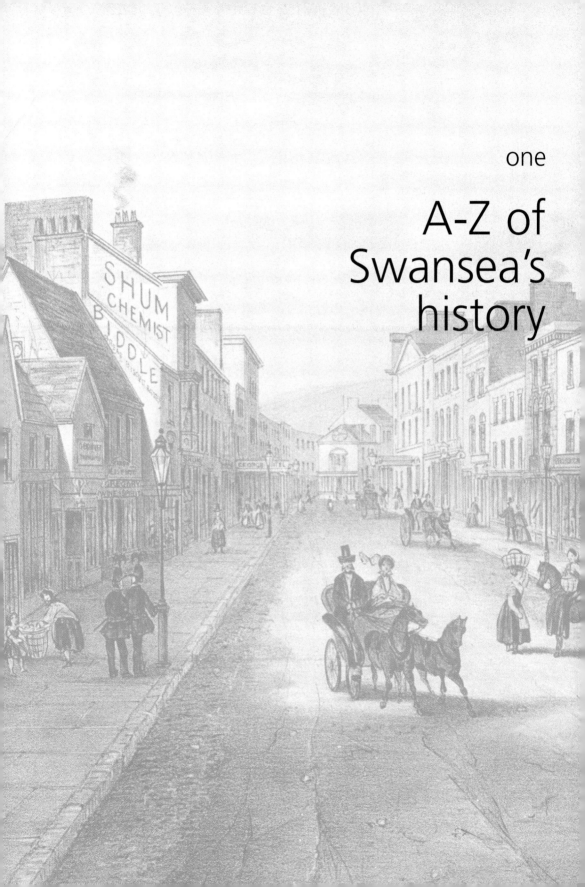

one

A-Z of Swansea's history

Argyle church, St Helen's Road

One of the things that must strike newcomers to Swansea is the sheer amount and variety of churches and chapels that dot the city. From grand edifices like the Mount Pleasant Baptist church (1874-6) on the Kingsway to the simple façade of the Philadelphia chapel – built in 1867 by Thomas Thomas (1817-88), one of Wales's most prolific chapel architects – still to be found on Neath Road, there is a startling diversity.

A devastating fire recently gutted one of the city's most distinctive ecclesiastical buildings: the Argyle Presbyterian church of Wales on St Helen's Road, built by the Swansea architect Alfred Bucknall of Sketty in 1873. Although a Grade II listed building, it closed as a church in the early 1990s and its interior was stripped out with architectural salvage and, ultimately, redevelopment in mind. It was built to accommodate 900 worshippers, which gives you some

The Argyle church in dereliction after the fire in 2004.

St Andrew's United Reformed Church, a distinctive city landmark with its twin flanking towers.

idea of the pulling-power of religion in nineteenth-century Swansea. This was at a time when the town's population stood at 51,000. The Argyle's grand classical façade is faced in Bath stone and measures 76ft (23.165m) by 50ft (15.240m) and the whole building cost between £4,000 and £5,000. Interestingly, the Argyle was built during the great Swansea chapel boom of 1870-90, when twenty-five chapels were built, five in 1875 alone. The Argyle church is shown as a Methodist chapel on the 1876-7 Ordnance Survey plan. You can find further references to the Argyle church in *The Builder* magazine of 11 October 1873, page 814.

Coincidentally, another St Helen's Road church caught fire at the same time as the Argyle: St Andrew's United Reformed Church, designed by John Dickson in 1862-64. Possessed of twin flanking towers that are square in plan but octagonal at the top, its construction was financed by Scottish drapers.

Baron Spolasco of Swansea

Baron Spolasco of Swansea (1800-58) was a quack doctor with a reputation that embraced southern Ireland, South Wales, Gloucester, London and ultimately New York. After surviving a shipwreck while crossing from Ireland to Swansea, Spolasco was most active here in the period 1838-45. He occupied a desirable Georgian townhouse where the *Evening Post* building now stands. Like many a quack doctor, he was essentially a con man who sold bogus medicine to the gullible. Spolasco was acutely aware of the legitimizing effect of newspaper advertising and in advance of any visit he always showered the local newspaper – for example, the *Cambrian* – with bogus testimonials to his therapeutic skills. He arrived in industrial communities all over South Wales in a grand open-topped carriage pulled by four horses. The intention was to create the necessary impression of an affluent, successful man of medicine come to town. He would then hold surgeries at the biggest pub and dispense his fake medicines to all and sundry – for a price. Always outrageous, he would walk his horse in off the street and through his Swansea townhouse after being denied stabling to the rear. In 1839, he stood trial for manslaughter after his bogus medicines were alleged to have hastened the death of a girl at Bridgend but was acquitted. Spolasco was even briefly imprisoned at Swansea gaol for evading stamp duty on his 'medicines'. By the mid–1840s, and with his credibility on the wane, he drifted away from Swansea via Gloucester to London and eventually New York, where he died and is buried. You can find out more about Baron Spolasco by reading the Stony Stories trail guide to the Maritime Quarter and by viewing the twenty-five stone panels in a walkway on Ferrara Quay that commemorate his audacious life.

Opposite: *A portrait of Baron Spolasco of Swansea rendered in stone, which can be found on Ferrara Quay in the Maritime Quarter.*

SHE
patronizes
merit.

NATIVE
or
stranger
far
away

SHE
will uphold
with
SPIRIT

THEN
brave boys
with
SWANSEA
honors

ALL hail...
SPOLASCO'S
merit

AND in
return his
grateful
donors

HE'LL
ever serve
with
spirit.

TUNE "THE ADMIRAL."

THE KILLARNEY foft 19th 1838

A detail of the sequence of twenty-five stone panels that commemorate the life of Baron Spolasco, to be found in a walkway on Ferrara Quay. Designed by Robin Campbell and Richard Porch. Carving by Brian Denman, Jonah Jones and Michael Watts.

14

Bascule Bridge

If you stand on the lower slopes of Kilvey Hill, immediately above the Addis works, and look up the valley following the line of the river, you can see a whole swathe of Swansea's industrial history. It is fascinating because it contains elements that span three different centuries and hence stages in the life of Swansea. On the skyline is Morris Castle, built in the Georgian period (1768–75). Below that, you will see Brunel's Landore Viaduct (1847-50), or what survives of his original design. Further down the river, before the new sports stadium, can be seen a small bridge that dates from the early twentieth century. Erected in 1909, it is an iron and timber bascule bridge (a bridge with a section that can be raised or lowered using counterweights) which is Grade II listed and classified as an ancient monument. It was built to carry furnace waste by rail away from the Morfa copperworks to new tips north of the Upper Bank Works on the east side of the river. Built for the firm of Williams, Foster & Co. (1893-1924), it represents the last of many such structures constructed to help convey slag waste from riverside tips that had become too big to use. The bridge tilted and opened to give the many sailing vessels that used the Tawe access to the wharves and quays that lined the river. Interestingly, it was not until 1887 that steam-powered vessels outnumbered sailing vessels entering Swansea Harbour. The bridge was originally operated by hydraulic power and had a water tank under its west end which, when filled with water, caused the main deck of the bridge to lift clear of its timber supports. This mechanism no longer works and the bridge is now fixed.

The bascule bridge as seen from the river. This photograph dates from the 1980s.

A rare photograph of the bascule bridge's counterbalance machinery, photographed from the river around ten years ago.

Bollards and the Swansea Harbour Trust

You can still see bollards most prominently down in the Maritime Quarter, where they exist in abundance. They rise up through the dockside like blackened thumbs or fingertips; others have flattened tops and look as though some great weight has slumped over them. Many cast-iron mooring bollards are still visible even though the industry that spawned them died out well over a century ago. You would expect to find them in the Maritime Quarter because of the docks but there are plenty left on both sides of the riverbank too. If you walk up the riverside on the west bank of the Tawe anywhere from Sainsbury's up to High Street railway station, there are still plenty to be seen. They are cast-iron memorials to the days when the river was the artery that fed the pumping industrial heart of the Lower Swansea Valley.

If you stop to look at one of the bollards, you will invariably find the letters SHT and a date inscribed on it. The letters stand for the Swansea Harbour Trust and the date conveniently lets us know when the bollard was installed. The SHT came into being in 1791 as a result of a Harbour Act which established a body of Harbour Trustees and empowered then to set about improving Swansea's port facilities. The practice of dating bollards was a marvellous idea and enables us to place most of the bollards in an exact historic context. For example, I recently discovered an old 35mm transparency of 1980s vintage that showed a bollard marked SHT and dated 1842. The date means it was in place before any of Swansea's docks were built, so this image is one of an early riverside bollard. Sadly, I suspect that this bollard is no more and only the transparency has survived. That bollard represented a tenuous link with what Swansea was like before it had any docks, before it had a river bridge and when its population stood at a meagre 24,000. In 1842, the Royal Institution (Swansea Museum) was only one year old and Union Street in the town centre had only just been built. When this bollard was first installed, Swansea was still largely

This photograph of an early mooring bollard in a scrapyard is probably all that remains of it. SHT stands for Swansea Harbour Trust and the date of 1842 means it was in existence before any of Swansea's docks were built.

a Georgian town and was in the process of losing its status as the chief coal-exporting port of South Wales to Newport. Nevertheless, in the early 1840s, half a million tons of coal came down the Swansea Canal from the valleys each year and left by ship. The area where the Maritime Quarter is now was still a residential area populated with Georgian terraced housing and was considered the better end of town.

The Harbour Trust thereafter went on to provide Swansea with not only a legacy of bollards but buildings too. Both Mumbles Lighthouse and the former SHT headquarters building on Adelaide Street – which was latterly refurbished as Morgans Hotel – owe their existence to the Trust.

There are still some important bollards that are definitely bits of 'history you can see'. If you go down to the rear of the Sainsbury's supermarket near East Burrows Road, you will find two sets of four bollards in an apparently haphazard cluster that look out onto some vacant land near the Sail Bridge. They are all in various shapes and sizes and all painted black. At least one is marked

These mooring bollards date from the 1850s and the patch of ground they stand on once formed one half of the entrance to the old North Dock, the line of which is demarcated by the curved line in the paving at the bottom of the picture.

This photograph was taken in the late 1970s, when the North Dock had already been filled-in. The bollard still exists and can be found to the rear of Sainsbury's supermarket, which was built over the half-tide basin approximately 20 yards back from this bollard.

SHT and dated 1858. If you look at the set nearest the supermarket, you will see that the ground around them is marked by a curved feature in the floor which is baffling until you realise that it demarcates where the old entrance to the North Dock was. These two sets of mooring bollards indicate either side of the entrance to the half-tide basin of the long since vanished North Dock, or Town Float as it was called. This is where ships came in off the river and sailed into a half-tide basin that had locks at each end. Once admitted, the lock to the river would be closed and the water level allowed to rise until it was the same as in the rest of the North Dock. The lock at the other end would be opened and the vessel then had access to the North Dock proper, which curved away from the supermarket and over to Parc Tawe. The North Dock was Swansea's first floating dock, which meant that it was always full of water.

You can still see this bollard submerged in the ground near a service road to the side of Sainsbury's. In the 1850s, the North Dock ran alongside it to the left, roughly where the cars are in the photograph.

Before then, ships had to moor at a limited number of wharves in the river (hence all the bollards) or in a natural harbour called Fabian's Bay to the east of the mouth of the River Tawe. It was where the Prince of Wales Dock is now. Nevertheless, even this dried out for two hours either side of low tide and all vessels came to rest on the mud and were hence unreachable for loading and unloading purposes. The North Dock was the first dock to be built and was created by enclosing the old curved course of the Tawe using locks and creating a new course for it by excavating a straighter New Cut. This took place between 1842 and 1845, although curiously North Dock did not open until 1852. With a breathtaking confidence in what they wanted, the Victorians decided that the future prospects of the town were best served by decisively altering the course of the River Tawe and using the landfill generated from excavating the New Cut to create land in Fabian's Bay.

Capel y Cwm Chapel, Bonymaen

This lovely old building sadly featured in a front page story in the *Evening Post* newspaper on 17 April 2001 because it was burnt out in a fire. It has remained derelict ever since and is scheduled for demolition, so see it while you can. It was a Calvinistic Methodist chapel called Salem, which means 'peace'. Built originally in 1782-3, it was altered and extended over the years before meeting its fate nearly four years ago.

As an interesting sidelight, although there are thought to be between 4,500 and 6,000 chapels in Wales, only something like 385 are listed and therefore protected. Of that number, only sixteen are listed Grade I or II. By contrast, there are 1,600 churches in Wales and over half are listed, with 60 per cent of them listed Grade I or II. The Bethesda Baptist chapel on High Street, with its distinctive porch, has been converted into flats and is one of only sixteen Grade I chapels in Wales.

Capel y Cwm's location in Bonymaen was chosen because it was wooded and out of sight of travellers on the main highway. It was for this precise reason that 'the ungodly men of the area would gather on a Sunday to play games, have cockfighting and every sort of merrymaking' there. Obtained on a lease, the first Capel y Cwm was built in 1782-3; forty years later, in 1822, the need arose to expand it. According to the edited version of Ivor Griffiths' English translation of *History of the Methodists in West Glamorgan* by Revd Samuel W. Samlet Williams (published in 1915), Capel y Cwm was 'pulled down and a stronger and larger building was built in its place'. Ten years later, a gallery was added around the interior and, again according to Revd Samlet William's book, the roof was raised by 6ft in 1869. The rebuilding that took place in 1822 and 1832 was paid for by contributions from parishioners, an amazing undertaking when you think of the circumstances of the congregation. The architect is thought to have been John Humphrey, who was from Morriston. He was not a trained architect and started out as a carpenter and joiner.

The burnt-out shell of Capel y Cwm in Bonymaen, still a fine example of late Georgian chapel architecture.

Copper Slag Blocks

They say 'scratch the ground in Gloucester and you'll find some history '. The same can be said of Swansea, especially for the period of the Industrial Revolution. Many artefacts from Swansea's nineteenth-century heyday have survived into the twenty-first century and one such artefact is the humble copper slag block.

These blocks were created using moulds positioned alongside the furnaces to capture the unwanted slag that was drawn off during the copper refining process. Hard objects made of iron oxide, they represent perhaps the first manufactured attempt at a cheap alternative to brick and are technically the Victorian precursor to the concrete block. No firm date can be given for when they started to be used as a building material in Swansea, although Morris Castle was conceivably the first instance, in the 1770s. The blocks were used as much as concrete blocks are today, for emample for large stretches of wall where visual quality is not important. As a building material, it was too dark and bleak for anything else. Naturally, the supply of the product was inextricably linked to the volume of copper ore being smelted, of which it was the happiest by-product. It never became a prestige building material and was only used sparingly in the construction of coppermasters' villas, housing, chapels or churches. Where it did achieve widespread use was as coping stones on park and garden walls and examples are still abundant. In Morriston, there are entire garden walls made from sizeable rectangular blocks of the stuff.

Here you can see two different types of copper slag blocks used in a garden wall at Grenfelltown. The half-round block was commonly used as a coping stone. These blocks can be anything from 100-150 years old.

The commonest shape in Swansea is a half-round block and there are also triangular versions, but seldom anything more complex. To see surviving copper slag block walls, go to the Hafod (an old copperworkers' township) and look at the garden walls around Vivian Street and the Neath Road area.

Empire Theatre

The next time you walk down Nelson Street on your way to the Quadrant, shoot a glance at a narrow service lane between two sets of buildings, for between a popular sandwich bar and a now defunct bookshop is an oddly shaped covered alley leading to a small service yard. What you are looking at is a surviving element of the long since demolished Empire Music Hall (1899–1960) that fronted Oxford Street. Its next-door neighbour was the Carlton, an early showpiece cinema built in 1913-14 by C.T. Ruthen that still survives, albeit as a bookshop. Construction of the Empire began in 1899 and it opened on 10 December 1900 with Miss Ida Rene as the main act. It was designed by Mr Walter Emden and the aim was to create 'a building that will dominate Swansea's skyline with elegance'. Unfortunately, it was described in its day as 'massive rather than charming' and cost £40,000 to build, most of which was spent on its interior. It had a colour scheme of cream, gold and electric blue and the quality of its

This tall rectangular entrance to a small service yard is all that remains of the former Empire Theatre on Oxford Street.

plasterwork could match anything in London, as was intended. However, the writing was on the wall for the Empire – and music hall in general – as early as 1896, the year when Swansea's first moving picture show, or bioscope, was held at the Palace Theatre on High Street. The 1930s were a watershed for music halls and they closed in droves as cinema grew in popularity. The Empire held its last show – the pantomime *Jack and the Beanstalk* – on 15 February 1957. The show was sold out months in advance. The Empire was knocked down a few years later and all that physically remains is this entrance, known as the scene dock, where props and scenery were brought in off Nelson Street.

Fish Weirs in Swansea Bay

There is 'history you can see' and there is history that you have to look for a bit. I am told that on a clear day at low tide you can see fish weirs from Heathfield Road above the city centre. You can also see them from the air and on the Swansea Bay Intertidal Survey Map 2, which shows the section from Brynmill to the River Tawe. The fish weirs or fish traps are strange V-shaped formations in the foreshore of the bay that are neither the work of tidal action nor any form of marine life but the work of man.

They are the most easily overlooked historic features in this book and perhaps the most elusive. There are four groups of fish weirs, or fish traps, in Swansea Bay, firstly a cluster of six interlinked weirs between County Hall and the Guildhall, at a distance of 550m-650m from the present high-water mark. To the west is a second group of six, at a distance of 850m-900m from the sea wall.

Post-medieval fish weirs in Swansea Bay, as revealed by aerial photography. They are the two V-shaped marks visible on the beach in the middle of the picture (Crown Copyright: RCAHMW Hawlfraint y Goron: Comisiwn Brehinol Henebion Cymru).

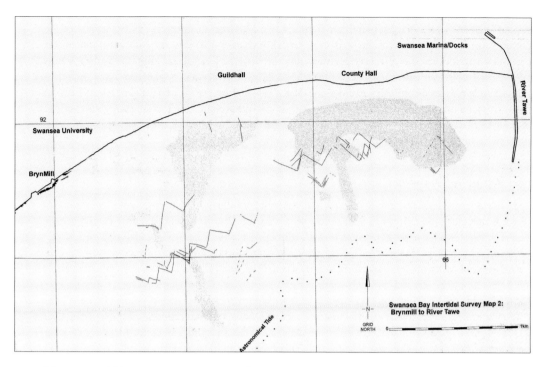

The position of fish weirs in Swansea Bay, according to the Swansea Bay Intertidal Survey Map 2 (Copyright Glamorgan Gwent Archaeological Trust Ltd).

Behind this group, at a distance of 350m from the sea wall, can be found a third group of two adjoining fish weirs. There is a fourth and much smaller set to be found on the foreshore, roughly a kilometre off Oystermouth. The earliest recorded documentation for the existence of fish weirs on the foreshore of the western side of Swansea Bay can be traced back to the sixteenth and seventeenth centuries. Certainly, mention of them can be found in a Cromwellian survey of the Manor of Oystermouth dated 1650 and a reference is made to what is thought to be fishing weirs in a 1583 survey of Gower Anglicana. There are even thought to have been fish weirs set up on the foreshore, where the Prince of Wales Dock now is, in 1656. Four weirs are thought to have been positioned on the sands opposite St Thomas' chapel, with the intention of catching shoaling salmon.

So what is a fish weir? It is a method of catching fish without leaving dry land or using a boat. A fish weir is basically a V-shaped structure made from posts sunk into the sand, with the space between the posts filled with either stones to a thickness of 1m or 2m or wattle fencing 2m high. With fencing, the incoming tide would pass through, trapping any luckless fish within once the tide began to recede. Using the stone infill method, the tide would simply flow over the walls, carrying the fish into the weir then leaving them trapped within a stone pool as it receded. The arms of the V-shape would be set at an angle of roughly 60°-90° and would be roughly 150m-200m long. Think of the V as a funnel in which to trap fish. Near the apex of the two inward-leading arms of the fish weir, near the low-water mark, would have been a large closely woven conical basket or net. The entrance to this basket, effectively a 'keep net' for the live fish, would be facing the inside of the weir. Fish would swim into the elongated arms of the fish weir and, unless they were clever enough to turn around and swim out, remain there as the tide ebbed, becoming trapped. Interestingly, for reasons never satisfactorily explained, it was common practice for the two arms of a single fish weir to be owned by different people. This perhaps occurred due to inheritance. To complicate matters, if someone other than the owners wanted to fish the weir, they would presumably have had to obtain a lease from each owner of the weir's two arms. From advertisements in the *Cambrian* newspaper of the day, it can be seen that fish weirs often came with property. In other advertisements, the wording suggests that the owners of certain weirs rented them on an annual basis. This suggests that fishermen rented them from the owners of the property rather than owned them outright.

You can find additional period information about fish weirs by looking at an essay submitted to the National Eisteddfod in 1884 (Davies, 1885):

> Between the Mumbles and Swansea a good deal of fishing goes on, but chiefly by means of weirs and fixed nets. Of the former there are thirteen, and of the latter three, or sixteen altogether; and the owners are very tenacious of their current rights. The bottom of the bay outside these weirs is, naturally a clean sand with patches of mud. Cod, conger, bass, mullet, whiting, soles and plaice are taken here with a few brill, turbot and salmon.

However, even by the time this was written in 1884, a decrease in the quantity of fish being caught had been noticed. This was attributed to a number of factors: the indiscriminate nature of this type of fishing, which caught all fish regardless of age or size; the dredging operations needed to create new docks; and the pollution created by the burgeoning metallurgical industries of the Lower Swansea Valley. As late as 1904, you could still see working fish weirs off Mumbles from the railway. Although by then they had been converted to the use of stake nets rather than wattle fencing. In 1935, the South Wales Sea Fisheries District Committee commented that the fish weirs now only caught something like 50 per cent of the quantity they took only thirty years before. Species such as cod, skate, ling and sole were no longer being taken. The fishing weirs were thought to be capable of taking roughly 1 ½ cwt of fish on each tide, with a total market value of £5. Observers can still recall seeing them in their characteristic V pattern on the foreshore as late as 1948-50. One theory as to why they fell out of use is that, in addition to over-fishing, pollution and encroachment, unscrupulous people used to steal fish from the weirs before the fisherman could come and empty them.

You won't find the fish weirs marked on any Admiralty Charts for Swansea Bay. Their presence can only be revealed by aerial photography and by knowing where to look on old maps and documents such as old estate surveys and accounts of disputes. While the origin of the fish weir or fish trap is possibly medieval, the reason for their decline and fall has a positively modern ring to it.

Grenfelltown

The stamp of history in Swansea often bears the maker's name. By that I mean the man that built and paid for an area's school, church or houses invariably conferred his name on them. The streets of twenty-first century Swansea still resound with the names of the Victorian coppermasters who brought both industrial wealth and pollution with them. Think of Morriston, Vivianstown/ Hafod and Grenfelltown. The remnants of the latter industrial village can still be seen on the steep slopes of Kilvey Hill. The Victorian coppermasters of Swansea were quick to build housing for their key workers once they realised they could retain their services longer with the offer of accommodation to rent. As early as 1806, schools were also being established and paid for by stoppages of 1d a week from the workers' wages.

The Upper and Middle Bank copperworks were operational between 1804 and 1892 and were run by the Grenfells, who had Cornish origins. At some point between 1799 and 1813, the Grenfells built three rows of terraces for their workers. The terraces step neatly down the hillside and, remarkably, can still be seen today, although they are much altered. Just look for three roads named Rifleman's Row, Taplow Terrace and Grenfelltown. By 1851 they had been christened Pentre-chwyth, and Pentrechwyth by 1879. They were designed without road access and water was obtained from a well sunk by the Grenfells at the north-east end of the terraces. There is a story, hopefully apocryphal, that a clause in the lease for these houses required the tenants to store their urine in jars for subsequent use in the copper-pickling process! Also built largely thanks to the Grenfells is All Saints church on Kilvey Road, which dates from 1843 and was the first church built by a copper magnate in a workers' settlement in Swansea. An earlier workers' village existed at Foxhole immediately below it but it was demolished during slum clearance in the 1930s. Despite their copperworks being significantly smaller than the Vivians', Grenfelltown nevertheless grew steadily in the early and mid-nineteenth century so that, by 1871, seventy-one terraced houses housed some 386 people.

The Grenfells originated from St Just in Cornwall and their connection with Swansea commenced with Pascoe Grenfell (1761-1838) in 1803 when, with a partner, he took over the Middle and Upper Bank copperworks. His partner dropped out in 1825 and the firm of Grenfell

Rifleman's Row as it is today; the houses are late Georgian in origin but much altered.

Taplow Terrace today. There are still remnants of what appears to be original garden walling topped by slag blocks probably made at the Upper and Middle Bank copperworks. The roofs look as if they are late Victorian and the top floor windows have been increased in size.

& Sons came into being and carried on copper smelting on the east side of the river until the 1890s. The Grenfells did not start living in Swansea until Pascoe's second son Riversdale William took a lease on the Maesteg estate on the southern slopes of Kilvey Hill. You can see what the Grenfells' Swansea home looked like on the 1876 Ordnance Survey map, which shows it sitting demurely on a small estate. It overlooks what was then the small village of St Thomas and was in clear view of the church at which the Grenfells worshipped. Looking somewhat closer at that old map, you can see that St Thomas was defined on its southern side by Fabian Street, which later became Fabian's Way. The 1876 Ordnance Survey map also shows that Fabian's Bay had not yet been filled in to create Swansea's eastside docks, and oysterbeds are marked perhaps 200–300 yards from the end of Balaclava Street.

Pascoe Grenfell's third son, Pascoe St Leger Grenfell, built Maesteg House in the 1840s and lived there until his death in 1879. This Grenfell threw himself into the civic affairs of Swansea and became a member of the Corporation and chairman of the Harbour Trust. Although a town councillor, he declined to become Lord Mayor. After his death, the company soldiered on for another thirteen years before finally going into liquidation in 1892. Perhaps the most benevolent and enlightened of the great coppermasters – by the late 1840s, he would not employ anyone who could not read or write – he built houses for his workers, churches, schools and even a music hall.

His name and that of his family endures in a series of street names and a park that can still be seen in St Thomas to this day.

Hafod and Aberdyberthi Street

If the imprint of history can be seen anywhere in Swansea, it can be seen most strongly in the Hafod. You can see it in everything, from the housing to the construction of the garden walls. Even the names of the streets owe something to the nineteenth century. Originally known as Trevivian or 'Vivian's town', the Hafod is the most complete surviving copperworkers' township in the city. The Vivian family started the Hafod copperworks in 1810 and the first housing can be dated to 1837-38. Those first two terraces can still be seen facing Neath Road and are divided by Vivian Street. They are remarkable for the amount of copper slag blocks used in their construction and in the garden walls. More housing was added throughout the period 1838-96 and St John's church on Odo Street was built in 1879-80.

Many of the streets were named after the Vivians. Odo Street was named after Odo Richard Vivian (1875-1935), Graham Street after William Graham Vivian (1827-1912) and Glyn Street presumably after Richard Glynn Vivian (1835-1910). Monger Street was named after Robert

This is Aberdyberthi Street in 1963. At the bottom of the street stands the Hafod copperworks tip; it would be another ten years before it was removed. The children are standing outside No. 25.

Above: *Aberdyberthi Street in the 1930s, before the Pentrehafod Road was interposed between the tip and the terraced housing. The tip lapped against the houses and crept down the road. The end house has had its slate roof cemented, presumably to stop dust from the tip invading the attic (Courtesy of West Glamorgan Archive Service).*

Opposite: *The former Hafod copperworks school built in around 1846 and still visible today on Odo Street.*

Monger, the works manager, while Aberdyberthi Street was named after Aberdyberthi House, the name of the works manager's house in the 1820s. This last street is one of the most interesting in Swansea, both for its location at the heart of the township and for its former proximity to one of the largest slagtips in Wales. It stretches from Pentre Mawr Road in the north to Neath Road in the south. The earliest parts of Aberdyberthi Street are the two terraces on the right-hand side as you look at Pentrehafod School, which were built in 1849. The rest of the street was built in three bursts, between 1850-67, 1868-78 and 1879-96. Aberdyberthi Street and the others that spring off it constitute an entire copperworkers' township, complete with a works school built in 1846-47 and St John's, the works church, built on Odo Street between 1878-80. The Hafod copperworks occupied a vast site sandwiched between the now defunct Swansea Canal and the River Tawe. A tramway from the works transported waste onto a site that backed out onto Aberdyberthi Street. Indeed photographs from as recently as the 1930s show the lowest slopes of the tip decanting directly onto Aberdyberthi Street. They were later regraded and the Pentre Mawr Road created, which formed a man-made barrier to the tip's encroachment.

The Vivians' Hafod township is defined by Pentre Mawr Road to the north, by Neath Road to the east and by Odo Street to the west. At any time up until 1973, the most obvious legacy of the Victorian era would have been the Hafod tip that soared 200ft into the air at the end of Aberdyberthi Street. It covered five hectares, was composed of 112,000 tons of copper waste and cost £400,000 to remove in the early 1970s. The Pentrehafod School now occupies the site of what was reputedly the largest copper slag waste tip in Wales. The Hafod copperworks existed between 1810 and 1924 and was once the largest copperworks in the world.

Half-Round Pond

Swansea is a city of well-kept secrets and one of the best is the Half-Round Pond in the Enterprise Park. This curiously named landscape feature can be found adjacent to the Wyevale garden centre in Siemens Close. Although between the months of April and September you would never know it was there because all views of it are eclipsed by surrounding trees.

The Half-Round Pond is roughly 2.5 hectares in size. It is a lung-shaped pocket park of great charm and is a haven for local anglers, who fish there in relative solitude for rudd, perch and tench. The literal name probably dates from the late nineteenth century, when there were metalworking industries there. There was a steelworks on the western side of the pond, although it was separated from the pond by a railway line. In 1899, the Swansea Hematite Company was operating a foundry and making tubes from an extensive works. The fact that there were sixty-four steam engines at

This is the Enterprise Park near the Half-Round Pond in March 1977. The Mannesmann Tube Works has gone and the London to Swansea train line arcs through the top of this photograph. In time, the Wyevale garden centre will occupy the land at bottom left.

The Half-Round Pond was once a reservoir for a steelworks; now it teems with all manner of wildlife and is a haven for anglers.

work in numerous mills would have contributed to the need for reservoirs with a steam pump house. The Half-Round Pond was, therefore, originally a reservoir fed by pipe from the Swansea Canal and also probably by gravity from the adjacent Fendrod Lake. The works operated as a foundry until as late as 1980, although tube production stopped in 1961. The works are perhaps better known latterly as the Mannesmann Tube Works.

The Half-Round Pond is a delight to walk around on a summer's day; its secluded nature belies the fact that you are minutes from the centre of Swansea and in the heart of the Enterprise Park.

Ice House, SA1 Waterfront

When we think of Swansea's maritime-industrial past, we invariably think of the copper industry and the Cape Horner vessels that plied a perilous trade between Swansea and South America. We forget that Swansea also had a fishing industry that pre-dated virtually all other forms of industry bar coal. Swansea had a native oyster farming industry in the bay that was at the peak of

Seen from the Sail Bridge, the late Victorian Ice House is immediately next door to Technium #1 and across the road from J-Shed, which is soon to be converted into apartments.

its commercial success during the 1870s. It employed 600 people in 188 skiffs (small sailing craft) that towed two dredges (a sort of plough that dug up the oysters) and landed an astounding 9 million oysters a year. However, by the end of the nineteenth century, oyster numbers went into decline and the industry collapsed. Then, as now, the familiar accusations of over-fishing, pollution (deforestation caused by industrial pollution which destabilised the surrounding soil, which was more easily washed off by rain) and disease were levelled.

By 1901, Swansea was also one of the centres of the British deep-sea fishing industry. There was a fleet of some forty trawlers, mostly owned by Consolidated Fisheries Ltd of Grimsby. In 1906, there were an amazing eighty-eight fishing ports in England and Wales. By 1925, twenty-five steamers operated out of Swansea, each of which stayed out of port for between eight and fourteen days and burned 8-10 tons of coal a day. By 1934, Swansea was among the top six ports for such fishing in Britain, the South Dock being allegedly given over entirely to fishing vessels. By this time, all the docks we still see today on the east side of the river had been built: the Prince of Wales Dock in 1881, the King's Dock in 1909 and the Queen's Dock in 1920. Decline once again set in during the 1930s, as fish stocks collapsed. After the Second World War, there was a revival as trawlers fished further and further afield, travelling to Iceland and beyond.

The fishing industry would have also supported curing houses, box factories, engineering shops and coal yards. This said, it becomes entirely logical to expect that there would have been an ice-making plant somewhere in the docks. Indeed an ice factory has stood on the east side of the River Tawe adjacent to the Prince of Wales Dock since around 1880. It can still be seen immediately adjacent to the new Sail Bridge and is a Grade II listed building. It was extended in around 1897 and became a chandlery in 1926. The ice was manufactured in the south-east side of the building, near where the chimney can be seen. There was probably a cold storage area for fish to the rear of the chimney and the freezing floor is thought to be still there beneath the modern floor. Permission is being sought for the building to be converted into a public house.

Japanese Knotweed

There are very few things around us that have survived unchanged over the centuries. Buildings, institutions and the landscape all fall prey to the ravages of time. So when one finds something that has survived and flourished for over 150 years and is as vigorous now as it was then, it is impossible not to have a 'creeping' admiration for it.

Japanese knotweed, or *Fallopia japonica*, was first introduced into Britain by the importer Phillipp von Siebold in the mid-nineteenth century. In Japan, it was known as *itadori*, which appropriately means 'strong plant'. It is now so prevalent that it is thought to be present somewhere in every ten square kilometres of land in England and Wales. Japanese knotweed can develop roots 3m deep by 7m across and can reach 2-3m in height. Its growth rate is of the order of 2cm a day. Mercifully, it dies back between September and November with the first frosts of autumn. Although now regarded as the most invasive and destructive of weeds, in 1847 it was awarded the Gold Medal by the Society of Agriculture and Horticulture at Utrecht in Holland. It received that award for being 'the most interesting new ornamental plant of the year'. Knotweed is the most adaptable of organisms and can survive in almost any conditions, from drought to high salinity, although it does not like full shade. It can now be found all over Europe, in the fifty states of America, six provinces of Canada, Australia and New Zealand. It has even been found in the chilly climes of Alaska.

The really fascinating thing about it is that research at the University of Leicester has shown that all the knotweed in Britain, Europe and America has the same genes. Genetic fingerprinting technology in the 1990s revealed that they are all identical. This makes all the knotweed in Europe

In 1847, Japanese knotweed was awarded a Gold Medal by the Society of Agriculture and Horticulture for being the most interesting ornamental new plant of the year. Perhaps they only saw it when in flower.

A fragment of Japanese knotweed as small as this can grow into a new plant.

The tiniest of rhizomes of knotweed swept down a river can end up colonising an entire riverbank.

one enormous female organism identical to the one that was imported in the nineteenth century. So when you next see some knotweed on your travels, it will be genetically identical to the plant that came over from Japan in the nineteenth century. It is in a very real sense an example of 'history you can see'. The first record of naturalised knotweed turning up in the UK was on a cinder tip in Maesteg in 1886.

Knotweed is a rhizomatous perennial, a single-sex clone and essentially one giant female herb. Normally, such plants need a male and a female for reproduction to occur but the European plant is female only. It has been able to distribute itself as widely as it has because of vegetative reproduction. That's to say pieces of the rhizome are the main cause of spread, as opposed to cuttings of stems, which are less likely to survive. People have unwittingly contributed to the spread of knotweed by trying to destroy it by trimming, burning and dumping it on landfill sites. Additionally, the creation of roads and railways has helped to promote the growth of knotweed because of the disturbance involved in their construction. When bits of knotweed fell into rivers and streams, they simply got carried downstream to colonise new areas or were taken out to sea, where they were washed up on beaches and promptly took root in the nearest sand dunes. Knotweed is generally sterile in the UK but can also sprout from fragments of rhizome as small as 0.7g in size.

The problem with knotweed is, of course, that it soon crowds out any competitor plants and takes over. It is nearly indestructible, requiring repetitive spraying with a herbicide over several seasons to get rid of it. The problem is the enormous network of underground roots or rhizomes, which are extremely difficult to penetrate thoroughly. Other techniques, such as mowing or tilling the infected site, are costly and labour-intensive and have to be maintained over a number of years to be effective. Knotweed is one of only a couple of species that have been proscribed by the Wildlife and Countryside Act of 1981 and it has to be treated as a contaminant by developers who find it on their land. It can grow up through concrete and tarmac and undermine anything from a river defence to a pavement.

The ever-inventive Japanese use knotweed to screen rubbish dumps and landfill sites, although you are advised to surround such stands of the plant with concrete, tarmac or brick. Research is underway to try and find a natural predator that can wipe out Japanese knotweed but until then we must try and control it as best we can. Little could Phillipp von Siebold have known what he was visiting upon the world when he discovered knotweed near his base in Nagasaki, Japan.

Japanese knotweed is not all bad news though. You can in fact eat it, although if you pick it from someone's land, you will need their permission. You can eat the newly emerged and untreated shoots – not for nothing is it called Sally Rhubarb – and it is even possible to make wine from it. Set out below are some recipes for cooking with knotweed. I must stress they are untried and anyone cooking with the plant should only use material that is untreated.

Knotweed Jam

4 cups peeled and simmered knotweed stalks
4 cups sugar
1 packet of pectin

Wash peel and simmer knotweed stalks. Mash and measure out 4 full cups. Place knotweed in a saucepan, add pectin and bring to the boil. Add sugar and return to a full boil for one full minute. Pour into sterilised jars and seal. Add mint or ginger to change the flavour or add to rhubarb jelly recipes as a substitute.

Almost indestructible, Japanese knotweed can even grow up through tarmac.

Spiced Knotweed

10 cups peeled and diced Knotweed stalks
4½ cups sugar
1 cup cider vinegar
2 tsp ground cinnamon
½-1 tsp ground cloves.
½-1 tsp ground allspice.
*In a large dutch oven or kettle, combine all ingredients, bring to a rapid boil, reduce heat and simmer for
60-70 minutes. Pour into sterilised jars and refrigerate. Serve as a glaze for ham or spread on crackers.*

Gonpachi/Itadori/Sukanpo

*Collect young Knotweed stalks (they should make a fresh sound when you break the stem off and it should
break easily). Peel the stems (soak in hot water if this is difficult).*
*Soak peeled stems in very hot water (80°C-100°C) until the colour changes (approximately 10 seconds).
Do not over-soak. Soak in cold water immediately and leave overnight (change water 2-3 times). Shake
out moisture and cut into short pieces (5-6cms) and sauté lightly. Add stock and a little water and a little
soy sauce/sesame oil/sugar to taste. Simmer for five minutes, adjusting the taste (do not over-boil). Serve
with rice etc.*

Apple and Knotweed Pie

For the crust:
2 cups wholewheat pastry flour or buckwheat flour.
¼ tsp salt
1 tsp dried spearmint
1 tsp cinnamon
¼ cup almond oil, vegetable oil or butter
½ cup apple juice or as needed.

*Chill all ingredients. Mix the flour with the seasonings. Cut in the oil. Mix until you have the consistency
of wet sand. Use your judgement to determine exactly how much oil or butter you need. Slowly mix in the
cold apple juice until you have a dough that's elastic and pliable but not too mushy. Press this into an oiled
9in pie pan. (A 50/50 mixture of liquid lecithin and oil makes the best substance for oiling baking surfaces.)
Save the excess dough. You can use it on top of the pie filling or you can freeze it for later use.*

For the filling:
2¼ cups sliced tart apples.
¼ cup sliced knotweed.
½ cup apple juice
1 tsp cinnamon.
1 tsp powdered ginger.
½ tsp nutmeg
¼ tsp ground cloves
½ cup sunflower seeds

¼ cup each black walnuts and English (commercial) walnuts or ½ cup English walnuts
3 tbs tapioca, arrowroot or kudzu

Mix all filling ingredients together. Prick holes in the crust with a fork, then fill it with the filling. Put excess dough on top, lattice style, if desired. Bake at 425°F for ten minutes, checking to see that the crust does not burn. Reduce the heat to 350°F and turn the pie pan so the heat is better distributed. Bake for another thirty minutes or until the crust is crisp and the filling bubbly.

John Jones Jenkins

History comes to us in many forms: as a large-scale artefact we see in the environment or as something altogether more portable. Sometimes it can take the form of a small pocket-sized New Testament. Obviously designed to be carried to and from Sunday school by a child, it is a humble little item with gold blocked edges to the pages and sturdy leather covers to the front and back. It is also an unwitting testament to the man named on its cover, John Jones Jenkins.

Sir John Jones Jenkins (1836-1915) was a remarkable individual who rose from the humblest of origins to become Lord Mayor of Swansea on three occasions – 1869-70, 1879-80 and 1880-81

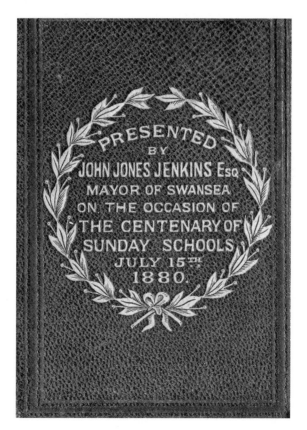

The cover of the New Testament bearing the name of John Jones Jenkins.

– and MP for Carmarthen District from 1882-86 and again in 1895 as a Liberal Unionist. Born in Clydach, he started work as a tinplate boy at the Upper Forest tinworks at the age of fourteen and became its outdoor manager at the age of twenty-three. In the classic tradition of Welsh self-improvement, he went on to set up a works library and introduced reading and music classes for his fellow workers. He also went on to establish, along with three others, the Beaufort tinplate works at Morriston and was a major shareholder in the Cwmfelin and Yspitty tinplate works. He was also a founder member of the Iron and Steel Institute of England and Wales. John Jones Jenkins was made a Knight Bachelor in 1882 and was created Lord Glantawe in 1906. Although known to have contributed to the building of many Nonconformist chapels, he is perhaps best known for being one of the driving forces behind getting Morriston Tabernacle built. Jenkins, along with fellow industrialist Richard Hughes, the minister and others, resolved to build what has come to be called the 'cathedral of Welsh Nonconformity'. They managed to convince another self-made man, Daniel Edwards, to build it. Edwards had worked for both Hughes and Jenkins until 1868 when he, Jenkins and William Williams established the Worcester tinplate works. Edwards stayed a partner for two years before dissolving the partnership to build Morriston Tabernacle. A foundation stone was laid in 1870 and the 1,450-seat chapel was opened three days before Christmas 1872. Its cost is disputed and ranges from £8-15,000, depending on which source you look at. The architect was John Humphrey of Morriston, who was taken with the minister on a tour of the most impressive chapels in England before putting pencil to paper. Hughes himself oversaw the construction of what was really an Italian temple in the heart of industrial South Wales.

Sir John Jones Jenkins led one of those Victorian lives that were full of apparently effortless achievement and selfless public service. He also found time to be a Justice of the Peace, Deputy Lieutenant of Glamorganshire and High Sheriff in 1889. He was also president of the Royal Institution in 1889-90, chairman of the Swansea Harbour Trust and chairman of the Swansea Metal Exchange.

A watercolour painting by W. Campion of Neath which shows the opening of South Dock in 1859. Almost all of the significant buildings depicted were designed by William Jernegan.

In Cambrian Place you can see a fine example of what a terrace of Georgian townhouses looked like.

William Jernegan

The architecture of Victorian and Edwardian Swansea still dominates the built environment of the city, even five years into the twenty-first century. The surviving fragments of Georgian Swansea are few and are located in their greatest concentration in the Maritime Quarter's conservation area. The terraces at Prospect Place and Gloucester Place give us a glimpse of what Georgian Swansea might have looked like, although Cambrian Place remains the best preserved and most pleasing to the eye.

All of the above were built by William Jernegan (1749-1836), who was arguably the best architect in South Wales in the period 1790-1830. Recent research has shown that Jernegan originated from London; why he chose to leave there and make for Swansea is as yet unknown, although it is generally acknowledged that the Leicestershire architect John Johnson, who came to Wales to build Clasemont for John Morris, probably employed him as an assistant. Jernegan conceivably saw potential for an architect in a town with a fast-growing copper industry and wealthy coppermasters, and little trained competition. Swansea also enjoyed a minor reputation as a health resort at this time and was briefly known as 'the Brighton of Wales'. Before the arrival of the docks in the middle of the nineteenth century, the area where they now are was called the Burrows and it was in this direction that the town expanded to build its quality housing. It was here that Jernegan's first known design for a terrace dated 1779 can be found. What it looked like can be seen from one of Thomas Rothwell's engravings dated 25 March 1792 in the book *Thomas Rothwell's Views of Swansea in the 1790s*, which you can still find in the Central Library. Jernegan went on to build most of the quality buildings in the Burrows over the next thirty years. We know this because you can find illustrations done at the time of the opening of South Dock on 23 September 1859 that show a number of buildings that can be attributed to Jernegan. There is a watercolour by W. Campion of Neath which was subsequently converted into an engraving for *The Illustrated London News* of 8 October 1859. An example of the engraving can be found in the library of Swansea Museum and the watercolour is in the holdings of the National Waterfront Museum Swansea.

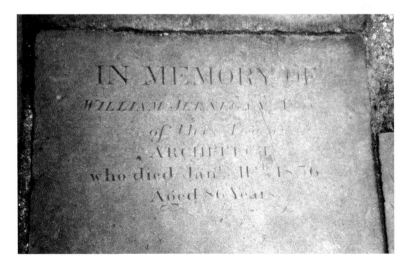

William Jernegan's headstone is still (just) visible today, set into the pathway around St Mary's church in the city centre.

This photograph was taken in 1847 by pioneer photographer Calvert Richard Jones. This rare early image of Cambrian Place shows how it looked when the Assembly Rooms (at centre) were flanked by two wings of terraced townhouses. William Jernegan designed them all.

Jernegan did of course build outside the Burrows. Mumbles lighthouse, Marino (now swallowed up inside Singleton Abbey), Kilvrough, Stouthall and Sketty Hall were all his work, in part or whole. Jernegan also built St Matthew's church on High Street (1823-24), which, although it has survived, has been greatly altered. In the Uplands at Eaton Crescent, you can still see a late villa by Jernegan, now known as the Stella Maris Ursuline convent. It was originally known as Bryn-Y-Môr and was finished in 1820. No original interiors survive, as it was burnt out in 1867.

Jernegan prospered until June 1811, when he was declared bankrupt at the age of sixty-one. History does not record what caused it, perhaps it was brought on by his involvement in the construction of the Assembly Rooms then in the centre of Cambrian Place. This project, which was conceived as long ago as 1805, was not completed until 1824 and was designed to create a social venue for the gentry and the coppermasters. Jernegan's involvement in the long gestation period of this project began in 1810. The Assembly Rooms cost £2,210 to build and first opened in July 1821, when 135 people sat down to 'a sumptuous dinner' and the evening concluded 'with a splendid display of fireworks'. All that now remains of his Assembly Rooms is its distinctive façade facing out onto Cambrian Place. By the tail end of the twentieth century, the Assembly Rooms had become derelict and were a boarded-up shell until the demolition of everything behind Jernegan's elegant façade converted it into housing. Nevertheless, every time I walk past the Assembly Rooms I experience a frisson of excitement at the thought of all the elegantly dressed people who must have stepped out of horse-drawn carriages ready to spend a refined evening there.

William Jernegan died at the ripe old age of eighty-five in 1836 and was buried in the graveyard of St Mary's church. You can still see his much-worn headstone set into the pathway beside the present building. The *Cambrian* newspaper, in a brief obituary of 16 January 1836, rightly recorded him as 'for many years the principal architect in the town and neighbourhood of Swansea'.

Landore Viaduct

I've always thought that Swansea has one of the most flattering approaches by train to any British city. Not for Swansea the endless chugging through bleak and faceless suburbs that blunts the drama of arrival. The London to Swansea line arcs across the valley floor, flanked on one side by the new sports stadium and on the other by the shining roofscapes of the Enterprise Zone. That it does so is due to one of the great figures of the Industrial Revolution and of the Victorian age in general, Isambard Kingdom Brunel (1806-59).

The Landore Viaduct was originally a 1,760ft (563m) long timber structure designed by Brunel. It was reputedly made from Canadian pitch pine and cost £20,000 to build. By 1833, at the ripe old age of twenty-seven, Brunel had become Chief Engineer of the Great Western

A mid-Victorian engraving of the Landore Viaduct in its heyday as it swept across the valley floor. Brunel's ingenious design incorporated four different structural systems. The Swansea Canal meanders through the picture at bottom right.

Railway. By 1847, he was in South Wales as the line from Paddington had been extended from Bristol to Cardiff. Construction started on the Landore Viaduct in 1847 and was ready for the opening of the South Wales Railway in 1850. Before that time, there was no direct rail link with Swansea that crossed the River Tawe. Surviving nineteenth-century engravings show a dramatic viaduct that used many different structural systems incorporated in one complex elongated design. The only surviving elements of Brunel's original design are four arched stone piers alongside Neath Road. The other piers and main central span date from 1888-89 and bear the inscription: 'Edward D. Finch & Co. Steel Builders, Chepstow 1889'. These are made from wrought-iron. Further modifications occurred when the eastern end of the viaduct was embanked and the remainder re-decked with steel fabricated beams in 1978-9.

Lockgate Sculpture

Looking for links with the Victorian era is not a difficult thing to do in Swansea and you needn't always start with something old either. If you go to the Maritime Quarter, you will see all the architecture and public spaces studded with sculpture or stone panels. Most of them were either directly or indirectly inspired by Swansea's maritime-industrial heyday in the nineteenth century. Details can be found in the Stony Stories local history trail guide to the area.

For example, if you go to Ferrara Quay, alongside the Marriott Hotel, you will see part of a lockgate built into one of the apartment blocks. This is a life-size replica of the lockgates originally built by the great Victorian engineer, James Abernethy (1814-96). The originals were installed in the dock outside the Pumphouse restaurant and were 12m by 12m (approximately 36ft by 36ft) and made from English oak, pitch pine and Honduras mahogany. Abernethy was appointed Chief Engineer to the Port of Swansea in 1851 and on 26 February 1852, the Marquis of Worcester cut the first sod for the new South Dock, watched by 80,000 people. It was to take seven years and many delays caused by lack of finance before Abernethy's South Dock was finished. It opened on 23 September 1859.

With the creation of the South Dock and the construction of a new high-level railway that came down from High Street to feed the dock, the Georgian residential area formerly known as the Burrows changed out of all recognition. For an investment of £169,073, Swansea's docklands more than doubled their vessel tonnage between 1851 and 1860, from 269,545 tons to 582,355 tons. By 1861, foreign tonnage had increased by 16 per cent and this heralded the age of the Cape Horner copper ore barques that would ply their trade between Swansea and South America.

Opposite: *The lockgate sculpture has been built into the end of an apartment block on Ferrara Quay. The designer was Robin Campbell and the stone sculptors Abbey Masonry and Philip Chatfield. Robert Conybear was the steel sculptor.*

Mayhill School

Of the many distinctive old buildings that still dot modern Swansea, surely none enjoys a more elevated position than the former Mayhill School. You can see that unmistakable curving façade nestled on the brow of the hill from virtually all over the city. Known locally as Round Top, Mayhill was an inspired place to build a school: 500ft above sea level and 1.11 acres in size, it seems to occupy a little kingdom all of its own. It not only enjoys commanding views over the city and the Bristol Channel but also the Black Mountains, Brecon Beacons and the Gower Peninsula. Although spectacular views are to be had, the hilltop position was chosen largely because of the obsession with open-air principles – the benefits of sunlight and fresh air – at that time.

Although from the valley floor Mayhill School appears circular, it is actually D-shaped with ten classrooms on the outer rim giving way to an inner ring of protected cloisters and a grass court inside that. A publication of the time described the school thus: 'the radius of the circle is so great that there is no perceptible distortion in the classrooms which, at a glance, appear to be rectangular in plan'. The flat edge of the D is formed by a block of supporting buildings comprised of two flanking wings of toilets, cloakrooms and masters' studies on either side of a central assembly hall. The site for Mayhill School cost £1,550 and it cost £15,155 to build. It was opened on 27 October 1932, in the presence of His Worship the Mayor of Swansea, Alderman J. Barclay Owen, JP.

As interesting as Mayhill School is itself, we should not forget the man who designed it. Ernest Morgan (1881-1954) was made Swansea's first Borough Architect in April 1913. He used to boast that he was born in the old heart of Swansea and that as a child he could see the arcade of Swansea Castle from his nursery window. It was perhaps this that set him on his way to becoming an architect. He was the eldest son of Mr and Mrs Edmund Leigh Morgan of Castle Bailey Street, Swansea. Morgan's training, like many architects of that period, commenced

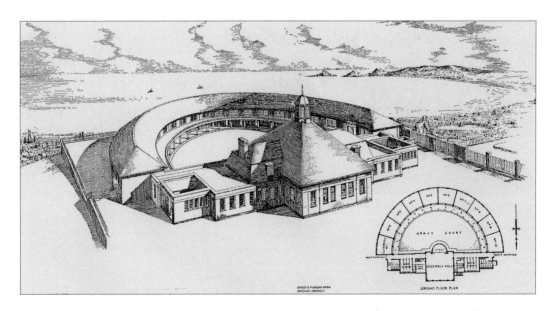

Mayhill School as drawn by Ernest Morgan in 1932. The drawing appeared in a leaflet issued at the time of the school's opening.

with a period at art school from 1900 until 1904. He was then articled to a practising architect in 1909. In 1910, Morgan studied at the British School in Rome and between 1910 and 1912 gained further professional experience in London. Morgan's professional career in Swansea began in 1912, when he won a competition to find a design for the Swansea Central police and fire station. The site was a difficult triangular one on Alexandra Road, on one corner of which Henry Holtom of Dewsbury had already built the Central Library and College of Art in 1886-7, which can still be seen. Morgan had to accommodate the police station and fire station on the other two sides and did so very skilfully for a young architect of thirty-one years of age. This work can also still be seen, although it is currently empty and awaiting refurbishment. It was while this project was under construction that Swansea Corporation advertised for their first Borough Architect. In April 1913, Ernest Morgan beat seventy-seven other applicants and was appointed. In a career that was to last thirty-five years, Morgan's architectural contribution to Swansea included Townhill Council School (1927), Mayhill School (1932), Gors Council School (1934) and Bishop Gore School at Sketty. His work was not confined to schools and he designed Cefn Coed Hospital and Hill House Hospital as well as some early housing schemes at Mayhill and Townhill. Ernest Morgan retired in November 1948 and lived at Ael-y-Bryn in the Uplands. He was a bachelor and died in a Swansea nursing home on 11 August 1954, at the age of seventy-two. The next time you glance up at Mayhill School, spare a thought for Ernest Morgan, Borough Architect.

Metropolitan Bank of England & Wales Ltd

History is revealed to us in many diverse ways. We look it up in books, archaeologists dig it up and very occasionally it is found purely by accident. At some point in the late 1990s, a shopfront at No. 27 Wind Street was being changed and the usual plastic fascia panel taken down. Underneath was a marvellous original carved stone fascia that had a tale to tell of Swansea's banking history.

The fascia bore the words 'Metropolitan Bank of England & Wales Ltd' in stone, and only a few of its letters bore any damage even though it had been put up in 1893. Despite the name, this bank had absolutely no connection with the Bank of England in Old Threadneedle Street in London. When this bank first opened in Wind Street in 1884, it was as a branch of the National Bank of Wales, which was founded in Manchester in 1879 and moved its headquarters first to Aberdare in 1880 and then to Cardiff in 1882. In 1893, the National Bank of Wales was acquired by the Metropolitan, Birmingham and South Wales Bank, which was originally the Birmingham Banking Company and had been founded in 1829. The early 1800s were something of a heyday for British banks, as there were no less than 800 licensed and unlicensed banks by 1810. They sprang up, usually with strong links to local industries or trades, supplying working capital to mine owners, industrialists and the like. The Birmingham Banking Company was renamed the Metropolitan and Birmingham Bank in 1889 and then the Metropolitan, Birmingham and South Wales Bank in 1892. In 1893, it became the Metropolitan Bank of England & Wales and was acquired by the Midland Bank, now known as HSBC Bank plc, in 1914. The bank in Wind Street operated as a branch of the Metropolitan Bank of England & Wales until 1909, when the business moved to Castle Square.

Thinking about Swansea's banking history, I was surprised to discover that the Bank of England actually had a branch in Swansea. This branch had its origins in the 1820s, when a banking crisis caused by a run on the pound saw hundreds of banks close as people withdrew their gold. The lesson learnt was that more banks would have survived if only they could

The Metropolitan Bank of England & Wales Ltd building in Wind Street as it looks today.

have called up cash reserves in time. To prevent this happening again, and to shorten lines of communication all round, the Bank of England decided to open branch offices all over Britain. Swansea's 'respectable gentry' were quick to petition the Court for a branch in May 1826, doubtless pointing out that Swansea, with a population of approximately 12,000, could call itself a market centre, seaport and seaside resort and was in possession of an industrial hinterland comprised of numerous metallurgical enterprises and mines. Swansea duly became the third of eleven branch banks that were set up between July 1826 and December 1829, seeing off competition from Cardiff, Merthyr and Newport. A Mr John Parry Wilkins of the Brecon Bank was made the agent of the new branch in July 1826. Swansea's branch of the Bank of England was not simply the only one in Wales but the only one outside England. It opened in the Old Bank in Temple Street on 23 October 1826 and lasted thirty-three years before trading losses led to its closure in 1859, when all its business was transferred to Bristol. The Glamorganshire Banking Company stepped in and bought the Temple Street branch from the Bank of England for £3,500 and moved an existing branch of their own into those premises in 1861. They were in turn taken over by Capital and Counties Bank in 1898, which in turn was taken over by Lloyds Bank in 1918. The Temple Street bank was subsequently destroyed by German bombs during the Three Nights' Blitz in 1941 and never reopened. Lloyds subsequently transferred business to its Wind Street premises.

This part of south-west Wales can also claim to have altered the course of British banking during the Napoleonic wars of the eighteenth century. An attempted invasion by 1,400 French troops led by an American took place at Fishguard at 2 a.m. on 22 February 1797. After a brief looting spree, the invasion force became too drunk to fight and was easily rounded up by local militia on 25 February. While the invasion failed comically, it caused nationwide panic and fear among commercial folk and triggered a run on the pound. People went to the bank to draw all their gold out in order to hide it! In no time this ran down the Bank of England's reserves of gold from £22 million to £2 million. Shortly after, and with the agreement of the Privy Council, the Bank stopped paying its notes in gold upon demand. This measure lasted until 1821.

Morfa and Hafod copperworks

If you frequent the Landore park and ride, you will doubtless be familiar with the large derelict building that overlooks the area. It is a somewhat forbidding structure that looks like some sort of Victorian school. There is even a clock tower to reinforce that impression. However, what you are actually looking at is the canteen building of the former Yorkshire Imperial Metals works. Built in the late nineteenth century, it was formerly the electrical powerhouse for the Morfa copperworks and is a Grade II listed building. Morfa was started in 1835 by the Cornish firm of Williams Foster & Co., who operated it until 1880. It was then taken over by H.R. Merton & Co. until 1893, when Williams Foster & Co. re-acquired it and ran it in partnership with Pascoe Grenfell & Sons (Cornish again) until 1924. In its heyday, numerous sheds of various sizes from which extruded a veritable forest of chimneys surrounded the canteen building. The Swansea Canal used to run behind it, the line of which can still be seen today, and both canteen building and canal were in the shadow of a 200ft tall stone chimney stack that was only demolished as recently as 1969.

Located 100 yards away is a long rectangular building that superficially resembles an old light industrial unit of a kind to be found all over the city. Used by Swansea Museum as a store, it is actually a former rolling mill and dates from the 1840s, when it was probably the largest of its

The canteen building in the late 1970s.

kind in the world. Interestingly, you can still see the walls of an earlier (1828) building retained in its eastern wall.

Closer to the river can be found more surviving elements of Swansea's metallurgical heyday, in the form of two engine houses fenced off within their own compound. These belonged to the Hafod copperworks (1810-1924). One was built between 1860 and 1862 and housed an engine to drive the copperworks' rolling mills, while the other was built in 1910. This contained a Musgrave Uniflow rolling mill engine; built in Bolton, it had a 29in cylinder that developed 600 horsepower.

To the rear of these engine houses, beyond the fencing and the shallow depression where the Swansea Canal used to run, is a track that was a roadway leading into the works. If you walk up that track with the engine houses behind you, you will see a stumpy structure to your right made of Pennant sandstone rubble. Almost unrecognisable now, this is the last surviving example of a mid-nineteenth century limekiln. It is missing its charging ramp made from copper slag, up which wagons full of limestone mined in Mumbles were drawn. This limestone was transported to the Hafod works by the famous Oystermouth Railway and by the adjacent canal. Anthracite arrived from the opposite direction, from the Upper Swansea Valley. There were once fifty-four limekilns along the Swansea Canal, producing lime for agricultural use and for the Victorian building industry.

To your left on rising ground you will see a car park and a building known as the Landore Social Club. This building dates from the late nineteenth century and was the Hafod works office at that time.

The Musgrave Uniflow rolling engine in situ, c. 1969.

Morgans Hotel, formerly the Swansea Harbour Trust offices

Located on Adelaide Street, alongside the *Evening Post*'s mid-1960s office block, stands Morgans Hotel. It is the latest incarnation of a building that was the outcome of an architectural competition held in the early 1900s to design offices for the influential Swansea Harbour Trust. Ninety-seven architects submitted designs from all over Britain with the sum of 100 guineas as the prize. This prize was not an insignificant one: 100 guineas in 1902 was equivalent to around £6,000 now. A Cardiff architect called Edwin Seward won the competition and Mayor Griffith Thomas, chairman of the Harbour Trust, laid the foundation stone on 18 February 1902. He did so using an ornamental trowel with an ivory handle and a silver blade that was presented to him by Seward for that purpose; the trowel can still be seen in the collections of Swansea Museum.

Seward, who by this time was one of the most distinguished architects in the region, had trained in Yeovil and came to Cardiff as an assistant to G.E. Robinson. By 1875, he was a member of the firm James, Seward and Thomas that went on to build some of Cardiff's most notable public buildings in the late nineteenth century. These included the Free Library in the Hayes (1880-82), the vast Coal and Shipping Exchange (1884-88) in Mount Stuart Square and a couple of the shopping arcades in the city centre.

By 1902, Swansea's maritime-industrial heyday had slipped almost imperceptibly past its apogee and the copper industry was in decline, with the remaining works refining copper rather than smelting it. Nevertheless, the town's population stood at a healthy 94,537 (it was 10,117 in 1802) and it shipped 2 million tons of coal a year. The Mond Nickel Works was established at Clydach in 1902 and, although by then outstripped by Cardiff and Newport in the coal-

The Swansea Harbour Trust offices, just prior to their conversion into an hotel.

exporting stakes, Swansea was still the key Welsh port for the export of anthracite, the tonnage of which could be measured in many thousands of tons. It is against this background that the Harbour Trust Offices were built; it was a time when the world came to Swansea. Among other things, it came in the form of the 1,996,567 tons of goods that entered Swansea Harbour from countries such as Mexico, Newfoundland, Norway and Spain.

When Mr Griffith Thomas officially opened Seward's Harbour Trust building on 12 October 1902, no one could foresee that within twenty years the country would be mired deep in economic recession. The Harbour Trust offices were an expression of confidence in a town that traded with the world and was confident of its place in that world. It was conceived as a showpiece headquarters built in Arts and Crafts baroque style with fashionable art nouveau details. Like many a headquarters building today, it came complete with corporate art, in the form of stained glass panels to stair windows, the interior of the ribbed dome and a large mural painting covering the width of the boardroom. This was in addition to ornate art nouveau light fittings and railings around the building. The first meeting there took place in late 1903 around a vast (27ft by 16½ft) oval boardroom table made from teak that rested upon twenty-seven 6in moulded panelled legs. The trustees sat upon thirty chairs made from solid oak and covered in crimson Moroccan leather that bore the Swansea Harbour crest in embossed gold on their back. The building's exterior is an elegant essay in red Cattybrook brick with bands of Portland stone. One thing about the building that always made me curious was the entrance let into its right-hand corner. It always seemed very odd that people were brought into the building via an entrance angled this way. Looking at drawings in the archives of Associated British Ports reveals all: the entrance led to a bank inside the building.

The symmetry of the main Adelaide Street façade is disrupted by the entrance to what was a bank inside the Harbour Trust offices.

Morris Castle

Perched precariously on a rocky crag on the crest of Cnap-Llwyd Common stands the remains of Morris Castle. Although dignified with the title of castle, it is of relatively modern origins. It was built between 1768 and 1775 by the local coal and copper magnate John Morris I (1745-1819) to house his colliers at the Treboeth pit. Twenty-four families were housed there in what was among the first examples of tenement-style living accommodation to be built in Britain since Roman times. Constructed from sandstone and ornamented with bands of copper slag with some brickwork, rents were being paid by tenants from 29 August 1773. The architect of Morris Castle was probably John Johnson of Leicester, who had been brought to the region to design grand houses for the coppermasters. Given its remoteness from the valley floor, the primary consideration was almost certainly one of providing his client with a picturesque addition to an increasingly industrialised landscape. The fact that Morris Castle would have been visible from John Morris's new home at Clasemont (also built by John Johnson) is surely no coincidence. History does not record what Morris's workers felt about the long walk up to Cnap-Llwyd after a hard day at the pit. Johnson's design certainly lent itself to being christened Morris Castle: it was originally composed of four square castellated corner towers connected by lower ranges – like battlements on a medieval castle – to create an internal quadrangle.

All that is left of Morris Castle today, windswept and partially undermined by Victorian quarrying to the right.

We do not know where the access stairs were located but it is likely that they opened onto timber galleries that ran around the internal courtyard. Each tower consisted of a basement and three storeys. According to an advertisement in a *Cambrian* newspaper dated 1811, Morris seems to have been trying to sell his 'castle' and by the 1880s it was in ruins.

Mumbles Lifeboat Window at All Saints church, Oystermouth

The Lifeboat Window really is an example of 'history you can see'. In October 2004, I was invited to attend a memorial service at All Saints church in Oystermouth. The service was one of thanksgiving to commemorate the sixtieth anniversary of the saving of the forty-two officers and crew of HMCS *Chebogue* by the crew of the Mumbles lifeboat on 11 October 1944. Stranded on a sandbar off Port Talbot at night and in heavy seas, the Mumbles lifeboat miraculously rescued everyone aboard, despite having two crew members in their seventies, another two in their sixties and a combined average age of fifty-five. For that rescue, the coxswain William Gammon (1900-47) was given the highest award of the Royal National Lifeboat Institution, its Gold Medal. During the service, I happened to glance up at one of the stained glass windows and was at once struck by the design. The window depicts the famous lifeboat disaster of 23 April 1947 when the Mumbles lifeboat lost its entire crew of eight members while attempting to rescue the crew of the SS *Samtampa*, a 7,219 ton Liberty ship built in America in 1943. She was on her way to Newport from Middlesborough when she ran aground on the rocky ledges of the Sker Point near Porthcawl. Her captain decided to try and ride the storm out at anchor but her cables snapped and in just eighty minutes she was sundered into three pieces.

The Mumbles lifeboat was launched at 7.10 p.m. and began its fateful journey towards Porthcawl. It was called the *Edward, Prince of Wales* and was the first motorised Mumbles lifeboat. It had been in service since 1924. All that can be known for sure is that the lifeboat reached the scene before being capsized by the sea conditions with the loss of all the crew. It was the first time that a lifeboat of this design had been capsized. The crew of the *Samtampa* also perished on that storm-lashed night, bringing the death toll to forty-seven. All the bodies were washed ashore the following day. The lifeboat crew that perished was as follows: Coxswain William J. Gammon, 2nd Coxswain William Noel, 1st Mechanic Gilbert Davies, 2nd Mechanic Ernest Griffin, Boatman William Thomas, Boatman William Howell, Boatman Ronald Thomas and Boatman Richard Smith. The Lifeboat Window depicts the tragedy of that night. It shows the capsized lifeboat in the middle of the picture and the eight crew members in the water surrounding it. Also in the design can be seen two segments of the *Samtampa* with the whole scene set in a swirling sea of blue and white glass. At the bottom of the window can be seen the lifeboat house, a village street in Mumbles and (I think) Mumbles lighthouse. Tim Lewis, who was head of the School of Architectural Glass at Swansea at the time, designed the window. For a piece of modern stained glass, there is a residual art nouveau feel to it and although the scene depicted is turbulent, the eye rests on it with ease.

Since the Mumbles lifeboat station was established in 1835, no less than eighteen lifeboatmen have made the ultimate sacrifice; many are buried at Oystermouth cemetery. On the other side of the balance sheet, the station has saved 797 lives and won nineteen RNLI medals, one gold, thirteen silver and five bronze. The majority of the RNLI lifeboat crews are volunteers.

The Lifeboat Window at All Saints church, Oystermouth, designed by Tim Lewis.

Mumbles Lighthouse

Its light blinks at us across Swansea Bay every night – Mumbles lighthouse is 212 years old in 2005 and still going strong. It was designed in 1793 (five years before the first American White House was built) by William Jernegan. The client was the Swansea Harbour Trust, which had been set up two years earlier and tasked with enlarging and preserving the harbour of the town of Swansea. A Harbour Act of 1791 gave them the power to go ahead and build a new lighthouse. Mumbles lighthouse is octagonal in shape and was originally powered by two coal-burning braziers lit by an individual who had to walk out at low tide. The prevailing westerlies made this a short-term solution and in 1798 they were replaced with enclosed oil lamps in a cast-iron lantern. Jernegan designed this too and had it made at the Neath Abbey ironworks. The lighthouse was financed by ships' masters who paid a fee to the harbour trustees every time they visited the port. Jernegan even designed the receipts that were issued and two can be seen in Swansea Museum. Having been allowed to visit the lighthouse by Trinity House (Trinity House was founded by Henry VIII in 1514. It is responsible for the safety of mariners and shipping. They are responsible for all aids to navigation – lighthouses, buoys and beacons, etc. – in England and Wales), I found that you have to climb a narrow octagonal stone stair to reach the lantern. A short vertical ladder permits access to the space around the lantern via a hatch, although it is very cramped inside. On the outside of the tower, an inscribed panel bears the date of its construction and the name of the architect.

We never think of Swansea as a Georgian city. However, Jernegan enjoyed a long and prolific career and was responsible for many fine and distinctive buildings in a working life that spanned the period 1775-1836. Inevitably, most of Jernegan's architecture was either demolished or altered by the Victorians, destroyed during the war or lost to redevelopment since. Nevertheless, you can still see surviving examples of Georgian Swansea, as designed by Jernegan, at Cambrian Place, in the short terrace at Somerset Place and at Gloucester Place in the city centre.

Right: *Mumbles lighthouse as it would have looked in 1793, lit by coal-burning braziers that had to be attended to every night. The captain of every vessel that used Swansea's harbour had to pay a small charge towards the upkeep of the lighthouse; Jernegan produced this drawing to illustrate the receipts.*

Mumbles Railway Electricity Substation, Mumbles Road

Surviving physical elements of one of Swansea's most cherished attractions – the Mumbles Train – are difficult to find. Apart from the forward part of an electric tram in an annexe of the former Maritime and Industrial Museum and the tiny bronze plaque fixed to the leisure centre footbridge which recalls the train, there is precious little else.

However, motorists who stream in their thousands down Mumbles Road towards the eponymous seaside village can, at Blackpill, see the railway's largest surviving feature. It is an innocuous single-storey brick structure with five round-headed windows that look out onto the road. Now known as The Junction, it is a café that caters to families using the Blackpill Lido to the rear.

However, when it was built in 1927 it was used as a stop for the Mumbles Train. Designed by Ernest Morgan, Swansea's Borough Architect, it was in fact the Mumbles Railway electricity substation. It housed two 500kw rotary converters that converted 6,600 volts of alternating current (AC) into 650 volts of direct current (DC) needed to operate the trams of the Mumbles Railway. This humble little classically inspired building was designated a Grade II listed building in 1998 and it took two years of careful restoration (involving the removal of its converters) to prepare it for its new use.

The origins of the Mumbles Train belong in the early nineteenth century, when George III was King (1760-1820) and the Prime Minister was William Pitt the Younger (1759-1806). On

The Mumbles Railway electricity substation today, in its latest incarnation as a café.

4 July 1804 at the Bush Inn, High Street (which can still be seen), Sir John Morris, Baronet of Clasemont, addressed the first meeting of the Oystermouth Railway and Tram Road Company. The occasion was to inform shareholders that a rail link was to be created between Swansea and Mumbles. Before this, there was no direct access between Swansea and Mumbles other than by walking along the beach. Not that public welfare was a consideration; the aim was to give access to the mines and quarries at Blackpill and Mumbles. Sir John Morris owned two mines in Clyne Valley.

On 25 March 1807 – twenty years before the Stockton and Darlington Railway came into existence – a horse-drawn carriage carrying twelve passengers plied between Swansea and Mumbles. The Mumbles Train went on to be powered variously by sail, steam, battery, petrol, diesel and electricity. Between 1927 and 1929, the line was electrified with 'cars' travelling at 7-10 minute intervals. These cars could carry 106 passengers. On 2 March 1929, electric trains took over completely; the first electric-powered service began at 4.40 a.m. and left from Rutland Street. The Mumbles Train enjoyed another thirty-one years of existence, with its popularity peaking in the late 1940s and early 1950s. It is argued that the steady rise of car ownership from the mid-1950s onwards contributed to the railway's demise, compounded by the increasing losses sustained by the bus company who were then running it. The Mumbles Train ran for the last time on 5 January 1960. So when you next pass The Junction, spare a thought for a mode of transportation that once carried in excess of 4 million people a year as recently as 1946.

The classical symmetry of this humble little building is a joy to look at; the architect was Ernest Morgan.

A postcard from the beginning of the twentieth century showing a very busy Mumbles Train, presumably on a bank holiday.

Old Head Post Office, Wind Street

We now live in the age of e-mail, mobile phones and the internet. Communication between people takes place in seconds, not days, weeks or months as it did in the Victorian period. Who now spares a thought for the niceties of composing a letter to a friend? Nevertheless, the postal system has left its mark on the landscape via the infrastructure of postboxes and post offices that dot our cities and countryside. Take a good look at them, they are both well on the way to becoming nothing more than a memory as they are either removed or closed down.

A former head post office can still be seen on Wind Street. Not the quite modern one so recently converted into flats with a pub on the ground floor but the glorious-looking building at No. 6 Wind Street that rounds the corner onto Green Dragon Lane and also has a café-bar on the ground floor. It was Swansea's head post office in the nineteenth century. Variously described as being 'Neo-Baroque' and a 'late Medieval Flemish Town Hall' (*The Buildings of Wales,* John Newman), it is a real ornament to Wind Street. It was designed by W.T. Oldrieve (1854-1922), an architect to the Post Office, who designed buildings for them all over the country. Built between 1898 and 1901, it first opened for business at 7 a.m. on Sunday 15 December 1901. The greenish facing material to its main elevations is quarella stone and came from quarries near Bridgend. The building was enlarged in 1916 and 1924 and even the loss of the four statues that used to adorn its parapet – representing Wales, England, Scotland and Ireland – has done little to diminish the impact of this elegant building.

The former head post office of Swansea is today a bar and restaurant.

The site of the building was also the location of another landmark structure from Swansea's past, the Mackworth Arms Hotel. This building was the starting and finishing point for the London mail coaches and was probably designed by William Jernegan. On the subject of coaches, Swansea's horse-drawn mail coaches were only superseded by train delivery as late as 1851. The improvements both in volume and speed of delivery can only be imagined. Bear in mind that in 1850 it took 3½ hours to get to Chepstow from Swansea by coach; nowadays we would expect to be in London by train in that time.

To understand why Swansea ended up with such an eye-catching head post office, you must first understand something about the history of the postal service in the town. In 1838 there were no sub-post offices in Swansea and but a single postman or letter carrier delivering 2,000 letters a week. To send a letter between Swansea and Neath cost tuppence, a sum too small to calculate in today's decimal coinage. In 1797 a woman called Mary John delivered letters and charged a halfpenny a letter for doing so. By 1822 a letter carrier was collecting letters, the delivery of which was free, at least within the town. This only applied to letters posted outside Swansea – letters posted within the town bafflingly carried a penny delivery charge. Also, the numbering of houses started in Swansea very reluctantly and the postman had to knock on each and every door in order to deliver a letter. Unbelievable as it seems, people were not willing to

This was Swansea's third head post office and operated from Castle Bailey Street between 1858 and 1901. It was not demolished until the 1970s.

(as they saw it) mutilate their front door in order to accommodate the delivery of letters. They were similarly reluctant to number their houses for much the same reason. The Post Office even threatened 'to obtain Parliamentary powers' to compel people to install letterboxes. Even by the late 1860s, the letterbox was by no means a common sight in Swansea. The take-up of a new innovation can often be slow as people take time to adjust to it. Cast your mind back to the introduction of postcodes in 1968. By 1983, it was revealed that only 42 per cent of people in Swansea could be persuaded to use them – the lowest percentage in the UK.

Back to the head post office, which always seems to have been situated in Wind Street. The most probable reason for this is that it was a nice compromise for business people based in the docks and casual users who lived in or near the city centre. The Postmaster of Swansea in 1821 was John Davies and the post office was housed in his jeweller's and silversmith business in Wind Street; he had a staff of one clerk and one letter carrier. The fact that he could run a post office from his own commercial premises demonstrates that there could not have been a great volume of business and that he could operate part-time. By the late 1830s, the existing postal system was both complex to operate and expensive to maintain. Under this system, the cost of every single letter was calculated according to its destination and weight. It took a man called Rowland Hill to point out that the most expensive part of any postal operation was not the transportation involved in getting the letter to its destination but rather the handling and sorting needed to calculate the fee. Hill advocated a single flat rate fee and suggested using either pre-paid envelopes or adhesive stamps. This led to the introduction of the uniform penny post and the Penny Black and Twopenny Blue stamps came into use on 6 May 1840. The fact that the urban population of Britain exceeded the rural one for the first time in 1840 was also timely. They say there is no idea like an idea whose time has come and, as a result, weekly mail deliveries increased from 11,600 in 1849 to 250,000 by 1890. The two years between 1847 and 1849 saw a 90 per cent increase alone. You can see parallels between the introduction of the uniform penny post and the growth in use of mobile telephones: in both cases, ease of use and an infrastructure capable of supporting the new service triggered a newly perceived need to communicate. Whether this need to communicate was real or imagined is another matter. The arrival of the postcard in 1870 only served to further enhance the attractiveness of the postal service.

By 1848, John Davies had been Head Postmaster of Swansea for twenty-seven years and still had another fourteen years to serve. By now, it was generally recognised that his business premises on Wind Street could no longer cope with the increased volume of postal activity. Temporary new premises were found in Fisher Street in 1849 and the head post office stayed there until 1858. Negotiations between the Corporation and the Post Office culminated in a new purpose-built structure designed by a local architect called Bayliss in the fashionable Tudor-Gothic style. Located in Castle Bailey Street, it stayed as Swansea's head post office until 1901, when it was taken over by the local paper and used to house its offices and presses. It survived the Three Nights' Blitz of 1941 when all the surrounding buildings were destroyed. The local paper remained there until 1968, when it moved to distinctive new headquarters in Adelaide Street. The new post office found itself out of date almost as soon as it opened; such was the growing volume of mail to be handled. A new site was selected in Wind Street, midway between town and the business heart of Swansea in the docks. It opened on Sunday 15 December 1901 and contained every mod-con, including (on the top floor) a gymnasium and a room in which the office's brass band could practise. The building was planned and designed at the very tail end of the Victorian period; Queen Victoria died on 22 January 1901. King Edward VII was not crowned until 9 August 1902 and the head post office is manifestly a Victorian building rather than an Edwardian one. It is also arguably the finest building on Wind Street.

Overton House, Gower

You can find Overton House in the Gower village of Overton, which is not far from Port Eynon Bay and the Bristol Channel. Overton means 'upper farm' and is probably English and twelfth century in origin. The village is bisected by a winding road that takes you roughly from a dwelling called Mere View at one end of the village to one called Windy Ridge at the other. Overton House is located at the heart of the village and is a seventeenth century former farmhouse; it is also a Grade II listed building. Listing documents indicate it had its origins as a 'single unit' home built in around 1700 and was rebuilt in the mid to late eighteenth century. There are later additions dating from the nineteenth century which include a bakehouse to the south-east end and a barn and dairy to the rear. Parts of the house date back to 1630.

The present owners are Gary and Mary Iles, who bought Overton House in the spring of 2000. It had lain empty since 1995 and no improvements or maintenance had been carried out since the 1930s. At the time of purchase, Overton House was roofed in corrugated iron and there was no indoor w.c., no bathroom and no water or electricity supplies. The house was in a state of advanced dereliction and well on the road to becoming an uninhabitable ruin. Photographs taken at the time of purchase show the sky peeping in through the roof in various rooms and a steady invasion by nature in the form of creeping undergrowth and water seepage.

Overton House vacant and derelict in the winter of 2000.

The exterior of Overton House in 2004 – with a new lease of life.

The present owners have spent the last 3½ years and their life savings to restore and preserve Overton House. A new roof using 3,500 reclaimed Welsh slates from a church and a school has been fitted. Tiles for the floors in the kitchen and other rooms were found in nearby fields, left over from the demolition of other buildings, and collected piece by piece for reuse at Overton House. Enclosed inglenook fireplaces were re-installed and the removal of much internal and external concrete render was required in order to restore wall surfaces to their original limewashed state. The civilised niceties of electricity and running water have been successfully introduced without loss to the cottage's period charm.

Perhaps the most significant feature of Overton House is a rare surviving charnel box, which is a feature of Gower buildings not usually found elsewhere in Wales. That you can find them in Devon perhaps confirms the English origins of Overton in the twelfth century. A charnel box is a recess above the fireplace used for hanging and curing food slaughtered on the farm or nearby.

Overton House was probably built by the people that wanted to live there, who most likely would have been employed in farming in some capacity or other. Skills gained in doing agricultural work would have included the repair of drystone walls and limestone quarrying and would have stood them in good stead when building a small cottage. Windows tended to be small for ease of construction and cost reasons. Roofs were low and bedrooms were built into them to maximise all available space; walls were rough and uneven because the stones that they were made from came from the fields outside. Such walls would have been made using lime mortar, as cement was not widespread on Gower until the end of the nineteenth and beginning of the twentieth century. The many limestone kilns that dot Gower are testament to this practice. Overton House's white finish is called a lime (white) wash and is used to waterproof the exterior of the dwelling. Applied year after year, it soon builds up into a coating perhaps half an inch thick. Timber would have been a rare and expensive commodity when Overton House was first built. Combing the beach for driftwood or shipwreck timber would therefore have been an important ritual for the first and the many subsequent owners. Of course, Overton House's original roofing material would not have been corrugated iron but a thatch made from straw or reed. The ironmongery that we take for granted, such as hinges and bolts, would have been made by the local blacksmith that every village possessed in those days.

The resultant building was actually a product of a number of limitations, when you think about it. Limitations imposed by the location and by the availability of materials and, last but not least, the capabilities of the builder himself. That we enjoy looking at and owning such vernacular buildings with their low headroom, uneven floors and walls and rough finishes is an interesting cultural phenomenon. Perhaps what we subconsciously enjoy when we look at places like Overton House is the outcome of countless decisions made over time in the building and inhabiting of it. Perhaps they are examples of 'history you can see' and that is why we enjoy them.

Pagefield House and the Quakers

You may be surprised to know that Pagefield House at No. 168 St Helen's Road was built all of 147 years ago, in 1858. This lovely two-storey Tudor-Revival building in red brick with pale stone dressing stands in stark contrast to many of the later additions. It is also known as the Quaker Meeting House; the Quakers were a religious sect that first arrived in Swansea as long ago as 1655 and have occupied four buildings in that time. The Quakers are also known as the Society of Friends and do not celebrate specific festivals, believing instead that 'everyday is the

The dining room of Overton House in 2004.

The sitting room of Overton House in 2004, a family home again.

Lord's day'. The Quaker Meeting House is a component part of Swansea city centre's Faith Trail, which takes in St David's Priory church, St Mary's church, the Unitarian church in High Street and the Swansea mosque and Islamic community centre also on St Helen's Road.

The Quakers had a significant impact on Swansea in the nineteenth century, as both ship owners and via their involvement in the copper industry. Dr John Lane of Bristol, who started the Llangyfelach copperworks in 1717, had a business partner who was a Quaker. The Cambrian copperworks of 1720 – the one built closest to the town – was run by Swansea Quakers. William Bevan, who was a son of the people who ran the Cambrian works and started the Nant-rhyd-y-Vilias works by 1814, was a Swansea Quaker. There was Quaker involvement in the first Welsh newspaper, the *Cambrian*; the founder, George Haynes, was originally from a Quaker colony in Pennsylvania. There are thought to have been many Quaker managers and agents in other copperworks throughout the copper industry in Swansea, even though their presence on the shop floor was tiny in comparison with other religious denominations. For example, in a

Pagefield House in early 2005. It was among the first houses to be built on St Helen's Road when it was still surrounded by countryside.

religious census carried out in 1851, there were only thirty-five Quaker workers compared with 3,958 Independents.

Swansea Quakers or people of Quaker origins had an impact in other fields too. In the mid-nineteenth century, Swansea was home to some pioneers of the new medium of photography. John Dillwyn Llewelyn, who was of Quaker stock, took many of the earliest photographs of Swansea and Port Talbot and was a pioneer landscape and botanical photographer. He took many photographs of his family and his estate at Penllergaer. His great-great-grandfather was one William Dillwyn, who emigrated to America in the late 1600s and was one of the first Quakers. Llewelyn was the eldest son of Lewis Weston Dillwyn, who ran the Cambrian Pottery from 1807, when it was bought from George Haynes, until 1817. He had a brother called Lewis Llewelyn Dillwyn (1814-92) who was an MP from 1832 to 1837 and founded and managed the Landore silverworks between 1853 and 1867. In 1883, John Dillwyn Llewelyn married Emma Tomasina Talbot, a first cousin of William Henry Fox Talbot, another pioneer photographer, this time from England.

Palace Theatre

If you walk up High Street, keeping the train station on your right and St Matthew's church on your left, you will encounter one of only two surviving purpose-built music halls still left in Britain. The Palace Theatre owes its existence to the Swansea Tramway Company that in 1874 was formed to lay tramways in the streets of Swansea. The company sold building plots adjacent to their tramlines to help fund further development of the network. Sales were slow and a Mr Almond offered to build a music hall in return for shares in the company. It was thought that such a valuable anchor tenant would increase land prices and bring people into the area. Costing £10,000, the music hall opened for business on Christmas Eve 1888 and could seat an impressive 900 people, all with an uninterrupted view of the stage. The architects were Bucknall & Jennings, designers of the Argyle church on St Helen's Road. Built in Ebbw Vale brick and Bath stone, there was an extensive internal use of concrete in floors and staircases, which led to the building being hailed as 'absolutely fireproof'. It was originally called the Swansea Pavilion but was renamed the Swansea Empire Music Hall in 1892. In its heyday, stars such as Charlie Chaplin, Lily Langtry, Dan Leno and George Robey all appeared there. In 1896, it hosted the first ever cinema show in Swansea. It was renamed the Palace of Varieties in 1904 and in 1908 was converted into a cinema. It was used for variety in the 1930s, was a cinema again by the 1950s and a bingo hall by the 1960s. Sir Anthony Hopkins was given his first professional acting job there in 1960 with the Theatre of Wales. During the 1990s, it enjoyed a new lease of life as a club; however, at the time of writing (2005), new uses are being sought for it.

Patti Pavilion

It is fascinating to reflect on what has to happen before an artefact or building can come into existence. Take that well-known architectural oddity the Patti Pavilion, for example. In order for it to find its way to Gorse Lane at the very rear of Victoria Park in 1920, any number of highly complex things had to come to pass. To start with, a female child, Adelina Patti, had to be born in Madrid in 1843 to opera-singing parents of Italian extraction. The parents emigrated to New York in 1847 in order to find more opportunities for their talents. Adelina made her first stage performance at the age of seven and by sixteen had made her operatic debut. The rest, as they say, is history and her rise

The Palace Theatre at the turn of the twentieth century. You can just make out that it still had its dome to the tower above its main entrance.

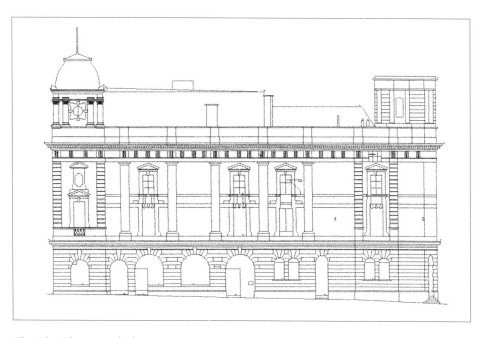

The Palace Theatre in side elevation.

to worldwide success was meteoric and enduring. By the 1870s, Adelina Patti was the most famous opera singer in the world. She made Europe her base and in 1878 bought Craig-y-Nos – which means 'the rock of the night' in Welsh – in the Upper Swansea Valley near Abercrave. Having bought this large early Victorian house, which had been built in 1840, for £3,500 (approximately £200,000 now), she then set about dramatically expanding it, spending £100,000 (approximately £6 million in today's money). For this she got a new north and south wing, a winter garden, a conservatory and a clock tower. It became Craig-y-Nos Castle. Such was the extent of her fame that she was able to pay for all of this with just one tour of the USA, for which she charged £1,000 (£60,000 now) per performance. The charismatic diva was arguably the most famous and highly paid female performer in the world throughout the 1890s. She was married three times, appears to have been universally liked and lived in high style. She even had her own lavishly appointed railway carriage maintained for her at Penwyllt station, complete with private waiting room. The local railway company laid on a steam locomotive to take her wherever she wanted to go. She held numerous concerts at the Albert Hall and raised large sums for local charities. In fact her last public appearance was in 1914

The distinctive form of the Patti Pavilion as it looks in 2005.

when she was already in retirement and seventy-one years of age. It was a charitable concert to raise money for the Red Cross. She died at Craig-y-Nos on 27 September 1919.

What we now call the Patti Pavilion was Adelina's winter garden and probably dates from 1891. She used to stroll around it with her guests and it was decked out with tropical plants and exotic birds. Old photographs can be seen in Brecknockshire Museum to testify to this. In 1918, she donated her winter garden to the people of Swansea. However, when the removal men came to dismantle it, there was no other labour on hand to help, all able-bodied men having left for the war. After her death, it was finally re-erected in Victoria Park in 1920.

The Patti Pavilion has been used for many things in the intervening eighty-four years. Most latterly it has been used for beer festivals, as a rock music venue and a temporary examination hall for the university. In the 1990s, it attracted the attention of a television makeover programme and was temporarily revived.

Port Eynon Salthouse

Salt, or sodium chloride, is one of the most important substances in the world, a shortage of which has immediate and dire consequences for both the individual and society as a whole. It is one of the most versatile of chemicals: it normally exists as a crystal and there are 14,000 ways of using it either directly or indirectly. In our modern world, only 6 per cent of salt is used for our own consumption; the rest is used by the chemical industry. Salt is right up there with coal, sulphur, limestone and petroleum as one of the most important naturally occurring elements in the world. Historically, its uses have tended to revolve around preserving, pickling, curing meat and fish and tanning.

This said, we should not be too surprised to learn that you can find a place for its manufacture near Swansea, at Port Eynon. The fascinating remains of an sixteenth- and early seventeenth-century salthouse and an immediately adjacent fortified house can be seen at the sea's edge. Located at the south-west extremity of the bay, you can see the roofless remains of the buildings and the reservoirs needed to capture the salt and heat it. This kind of salt manufacture is known as solar salt production and depends for its success on the action of sun and wind on seawater. At Port Eynon, seawater was collected in a series of three stone-lined chambers at the level of the beach before being pumped to the higher level, where the water would be heated in coal-fired furnaces and the salt separated by evaporation. The pump used to move water from one chamber to the next was itself a marvel of innovation. It consisted of a hollowed-out tree trunk 1.75m in length; it even had a non-return valve. Before the late 1980s, Port Eynon's salthouse was in danger of being lost to us because of coastal erosion and the Glamorgan Archaeological Trust excavated the site with a view to recording it before it disappeared. Such was the historic importance of the site that it was deemed necessary to protect it from further erosion and a low-level protective perimeter wall was built to stop the reservoirs from being washed slowly away. Port Eynon Salthouse is now categorised by Cadw as an ancient monument; its specific class is that of Industrial Site. If this seems a little incongruous given its Gower location, then you have to remember that Port Eynon was not always the deliciously quiet and picturesque place it is now. In the mid-sixteenth century, it was a hive of industry for the cross-channel trade in farm produce. Additionally, much of the lime burnt on Gower in numerous limestone kilns found its way onto farmland in north Devon to improve the soil. By the middle of the eighteenth century, oyster fishing was established and supported a fleet of forty skiffs (small three or four man sailing vessels). Such was the extent of the trade that by the nineteenth century the salthouse buildings actually became homes for oyster fishermen. Sadly, the last haul of oysters at Port Eynon took

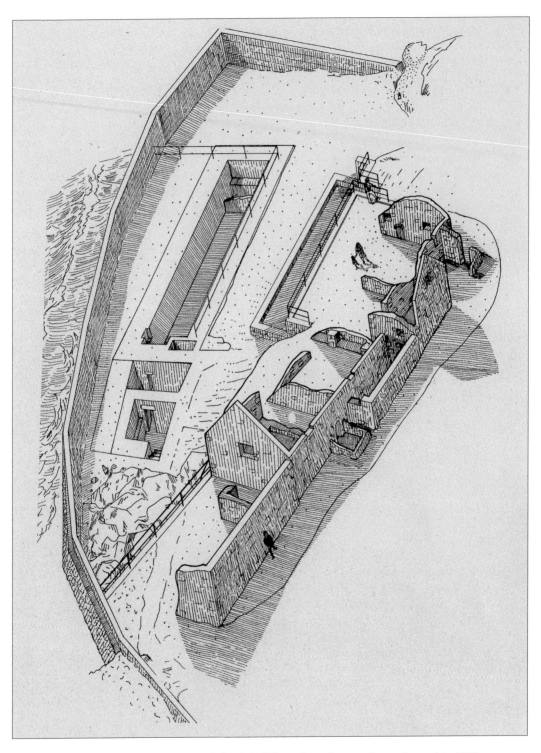

A drawing prepared by the Glamorgan Gwent Archaeological Trust prior to the start of restoration work in 1995 (Copyright Glamorgan Gwent Archaeological Trust Ltd).

place in 1879 and the industry went into decline. The oyster fishing industry of Swansea Bay and Gower gave jobs to hundreds of people and used to harvest many million of oysters per annum. A deadly combination of our old friends over-fishing, disease and pollution put paid to it until only very recently.

Prince of Wales Dock

The Prince of Wales Dock was the last of the three great Victorian docks that energised Swansea and made it one of the great ports of the nineteenth century. By 1870, the capacity of the North Dock, which had been built in 1852, and the South Dock, built in 1859, had been exceeded. By the late 1870s, the need for a new dock had become urgent due to severe overcrowding caused

Port Eynon Salthouse in the late 1980s, as excavation was just getting underway.

by the burgeoning metallurgical industries of the Lower Swansea Valley. The Harbour Trust purchased land on the east side of the river and the contract for the construction of an East Dock was let on 15 June 1879. On 31 March 1880, the trustees of the dock laid a foundation stone at a ceremony led by Henry Hussey Vivian. The 1880s were to be the decade of Swansea's greatest maritime-industrial prosperity. Its exports of copper, tinplate, zinc and coal were exported worldwide. On 22 June 1882, the Prince and Princess of Wales, later to be King George VII and Queen Alexandra, opened the dock, which was named in their honour. The entire population of the town – over 76,000 people – turned out to see the event.

The Prince of Wales Dock was in the news again more recently when it was announced that it was to form part of the SA1 Swansea Waterfront project. This is the name given to a visionary masterplan put forward by the Welsh Development Agency and National Assembly. The aim is

A detail from an engraving of Swansea Docks in the 1880s. The Prince of Wales Dock is the long, rectangular feature filled with ships in the middle of the picture.

to attract £200 million of investment and create a mixed development of residential, retail and leisure facilities wrapped around the dock. It is a well-known fact that the value of any property is dramatically enhanced when it overlooks water. A century after being opened, the Prince of Wales Dock will once again be contributing to the prosperity of Swansea.

Redevelopment

Up until now I have dealt with Swansea's historic artefacts, buildings or structures. However, I would now like to introduce some drawings, ones prepared during the 1940s with the intention of illustrating the town centre of the future. Plans to rebuild Swansea's war-torn town centre began to be made almost as soon as the tide of the Second World War turned in the Allies' favour in 1942. The Borough Engineer was instructed to prepare preliminary proposals for work to start

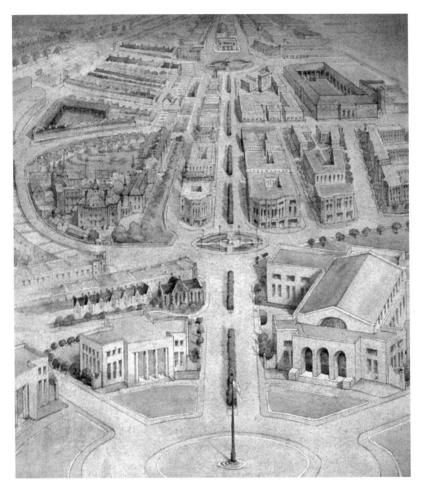

Right: *An imaginary view looking down a dramatically straightened St Helen's Road toward the Kingsway roundabout at the top of the picture. The viewpoint seems to be from the top of the Guildhall's clock tower (Courtesy of West Glamorgan Archive Service).*

Showing some nice examples of period motorcars, this is an imaginary view looking down the Kingsway towards High Street. In the middle distance at far right the Mount Pleasant Baptist church can just be seen (Courtesy of West Glamorgan Archive Service).

immediately after the war. His first idea called for a processional way or grand boulevard to link the town centre with the Guildhall. This idea was linked to future traffic control and included a kind of inner ring road. Scale models were made but this grand scheme was dropped when it was discovered it would have involved the purchase and demolition of more buildings than had been destroyed in the Blitz. Nevertheless, you can see a vastly scaled down fragment of this proposal in the form of the Kingsway today. Additional scale models were made by the Estates Department in 1944 and survived until the 1950s but are assumed to have been lost since.

Serious reconstruction of the town centre was put off until the early 1950s due to chronic shortages of materials. This, more than a lack of imagination or vision, explains why subsequent city centre buildings were constructed as plainly as possible. They nevertheless bear a striking resemblance to buildings depicted in the numerous reconstruction drawings produced during the 1940s that have survived to this day. Disappointingly, the prime motivation behind the drawings seems to be road layouts and traffic management rather than architecture. The original drawings are in the care of the West Glamorgan Archive Service at County Hall on Oystermouth Road.

This view looks down Quay Parade towards Swansea Museum, with Morgans Hotel on the left. At far right can be seen the railway viaduct that used to bridge the bottom of Wind Street and led off to North Dock; extensive sidings used to exist behind Swansea Museum at this time. The small structure in the foreground of the picture is an early public telephone box (Courtesy of West Glamorgan Archive Service).

Sir Charles Tamlin Ruthen

It is a sad fact of life that the people who do most to shape the city we see around us are seldom formally recognised. Architects design the buildings that frame our public spaces and give form and order to the built environment. Yet how many people reading this could name a single architect from either Swansea's past or its present. Few, I'll warrant.

Swansea has been fortunate in having a number of good local architects who have ornamented the city with their works. William Jernegan, Ernest Morgan and Charles Ruthen between them built most of Swansea's memorable buildings between 1790 and 1930.

Sir Charles Tamlin Ruthen (1871-1926) was English and arrived in Swansea having secured a job with the Borough Surveyor. He began work in the Swansea and Gower area in 1890 and was involved with the extension to the Mount Pleasant workhouse at that time. This complex of Victorian structures evolved over time to become known latterly as Mount Pleasant Hospital. It fell out of use and was successfully refurbished as housing properties in 2003. Now owned by Swansea Housing Association, the whole complex was re-energised by selective demolition, alteration and new additions. Located close to the city centre, it is an interesting architectural experience.

By 1896, Ruthen was in private practice in Bank Chambers, Heathfield Street. He also did some semi-detached housing at Sketty, at Nos 27-47 Dillwyn Road (1905), and two terraces at Nos 1-11 De La Beche Road (1906). These can still be seen, as can his Pantygwydr English Baptist church at Brynmill (1906-7). After 1910, Ruthen's career really began to take off as he built the Mond Buildings on Union Street (1911), Swansea Exchange Buildings (1913-4) and the Carlton cinema – now a bookshop – on Oxford Street (1913-4). All of these buildings have since been listed Grade II by the conservation agency Cadw and can still be seen in the city centre. They were all built in a confident Edwardian baroque style, basically a form of ornate early twentieth-century classicism. Both the Exchange Buildings and Mond Buildings were made of Portland stone. Mond Buildings was paid for by the eponymous Sir Alfred Mond (1868-1930) and was originally the local headquarters for the National League of Young Liberals. Ruthen was a member of the Liberal Party and Mond became something of a mentor to him. Mond was the son of Ludwig Mond, who in 1902 founded the Mond Nickel Works at Clydach, the largest in the world at that time before they were absorbed into the Canadian INCO company. Ruthen was the Liberal MP for Swansea between 1910 and 1923 and became the first chairman of ICI in 1926.

Perhaps the best known of Ruthen's buildings is the former Carlton cinema, now perhaps better known as Waterstone's bookshop. This really is the definition of a landmark building. Described in one book of architecture in Wales as 'a splendidly swaggering piece of baroque design', this has to be Ruthen's masterpiece. The client was the Swansea Electric Company and

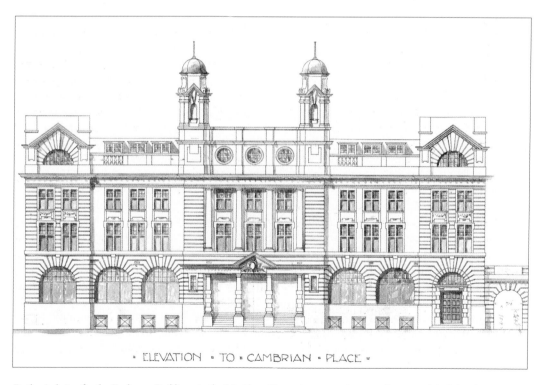

Ruthen's design for the Exchange Buildings in the Maritime Quarter's conservation area, from an original drawing.

the building could seat 600 on the ground floor and 300 in the circle. Ruthen used reinforced concrete in its construction to give a column-free view of the stage. Described in the *South Wales Daily Post* of January 1914 as 'the last word in cinemas', it was faced with Doulton's white Carraraware to give it an expensive-looking finish. The Carlton changed hands on many occasions but remained a cinema until 1978, when it closed and fell vacant. Seemingly destined for demolition like the Empire, it was rescued at the last minute when the City Council sought its designation as a listed building. The only element of Ruthen's original design that survived the conversion to a bookshop was the dramatic curving staircase that ascends through the full height of the building.

Scott's Pit Engine House

During the period 1850-80, Swansea was rightfully known as Copperopolis because of the extent of its copper smelting industries. Even when that industry began to be undermined by a combination of foreign import tariffs and the construction of bigger and more modern plants abroad, other metallurgical industries arose to take its place. Copperopolis became Tinopolis and, by 1913, four out of five tinplate workers in Britain lived within a 20-mile radius of Swansea.

Nevertheless, it is worth remembering that Swansea was also an important coal-exporting port. It went from small beginnings in 1780, when it exported a relatively meagre 65,000 tons, to 1913, when it exported 4.5 million tons. However, despite not starting to export coal until the 1820s, later than Swansea, by 1913 Cardiff and Newport were exporting 24.58 million tons and 6.14 million tons respectively. On the import side of the equation, that was also the year that some 5,832 steam and sailing vessels entered Swansea Harbour carrying 3.5 million tons of cargo.

Swansea's coal industry can be traced back to the 1500s, when it is thought only Newcastle and Sunderland could surpass it. The use of coal for domestic and light industrial purposes pre-dates the copper industry by centuries and output for it peaked as long ago as the end of the eighteenth century. At this time, it took three tons of coal to smelt one ton of copper, so the arrival of the copper industry in the early eighteenth century acted as a stimulus to coal production in the Swansea area. The early shallow and unventilated pits gave way to deep drift mines prone to bad air and flooding. In response to this, firms like Boulton & Watt and Abraham Darby of Coalbrookdale invented and perfected steam-driven pumping engines to mechanically empty the pits of water.

In around 1817-19, a London solicitor called John Scott sank a 500ft (150m) pit in Llansamlet that proved unsuccessful. He sold it in 1828 to Charles Henry Smith, a local coal owner of Gwernllwynchwyth who had earlier (1783-85) built a 3 mile long canal to carry coal from his pits in Llansamlet to the river at Foxhole. The curious-looking structure still to be seen above the pit is a Cornish beam-engine house built between 1817 and 1819; it was one of the first of its kind to be constructed in South Wales. It used to house a low-pressure Boulton & Watt pumping engine that was operated there until 1842. By 1872, a newer high-pressure pumping engine had been fitted and was used to drain the Cae Pridd colliery. It stayed in use off and on, as owners came and went, until 1930.

Scott's pit is worth a look because it is one of the few surviving elements of Swansea's coal industry still visible today.

Scott's pit engine house, 2005.

Second World War Pillbox at Swansea Bay

A literally concrete reminder of the Second World War can still be seen on the beach opposite the university. I'm talking about a pillbox built presumably in 1939 to guard Swansea against seaborne invasion. This pillbox was unlikely to have been used to defend the beach, as the window openings let into its sides look east to west along the beach rather than out to sea. It would most likely have been used as a lookout post, ready to alert the city's defences at the first sign of an attempted landing. There is a square, water-filled depression on the lid of the pillbox, which suggests that perhaps a forward-facing hatch once existed. Alternatively, it may have been a void so that a periscope could be pushed through in order to look out to sea. The pillbox's only blank wall faces out to sea.

This Second World War pillbox can still be seen on the beach opposite the university. It is an enduring reminder of the war.

The threat of invasion was at its height in the early years of the war, when the Nazis had a plan called Operation Sealion, which called for the invasion of Britain in 1940. Admittedly, the invasion would almost certainly have been focused around the Dover-Calais region. Nevertheless, there were German submarines active in the Bristol Channel. Fortunately for us, Operation Sealion was predicated upon the destruction of the RAF as a prerequisite to any invasion. The inability of the Luftwaffe to accomplish this during the summer of 1940 led Hitler to postpone the invasion indefinitely. However, if the risk of seaborne invasion was slight then the landing of raiding parties or saboteurs was very real – hence the need for a pillbox. It is thought that of the 18,000 pillboxes built in the UK before the war, many thousands still survive lurking in the corner of fields and dug into clifftops all over Britain. This is surprising when you learn that farmers were offered £5 to demolish any pillboxes on their property after the war. In addition to their sentimental appeal, some pillboxes actually have some real estate value, often due to their clifftop locations.

A detail of one of the two window openings let into the sides of the pillbox to enable the users to scan the beach in each direction. Time has weathered the concrete and the reinforcing bars are starting to show through.

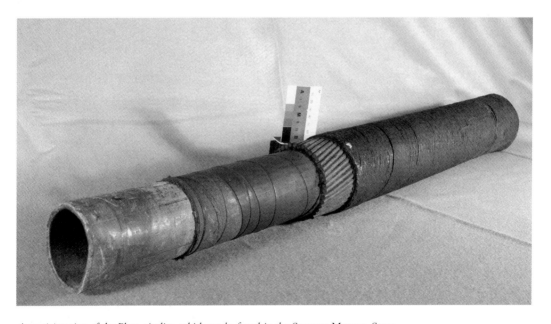

A surviving piece of the Pluto pipeline, which can be found in the Swansea Museum Stores.

In August 2004, a large south Devon pillbox came up for auction as a holiday home with an asking price of £70,000.

Swansea did play a more active part in the downfall of the Nazis via its involvement in the invasion of Normandy and Operation Pluto. Pluto was the acronym for Pipe Line Under The Ocean, one of the many fascinating inventions that were generated by the exigencies of the Second World War. The idea was to be able to supply any future invasion beachhead by means of a pipeline lying on the seabed. This did away for the need for vulnerable oil tankers to lie immediately offshore and to avoid further cluttering up the beach with vehicles and people. However, to develop such a submarine pipeline would need a new kind of flexible hollow pipeline and a vessel capable of laying it in one continuous procedure.

Initial trials of experimental pipeworks were made on the Clyde. However, Swansea was chosen to test whether the Pluto pipeline could work over long distances. To this end, a decision was made to link Swansea with the Devon village of Watermouth 45 miles away on the other side of the Bristol Channel via a submerged pipeline. A pumping station was set up on the Queen's Dock and 2,000 yards of pipeline was paid out from both the shores of Swansea and Watermouth and buoyed in place. On 27 December 1942, the appropriately named HMS *Holdfast*, a cable-laying ship, collected the Swansea end of the cable and steamed for Watermouth, laying it on the seabed as she went. Despite many setbacks, this amazing technical experiment succeeded and fuel was successfully pumped through an undersea pipeline lying on the seabed. The technology was perfected in time for the Normandy landings of 1944 and Pluto undersea pipelines were laid from the Isle of Wight to Cherbourg (70 miles) and from Dungeness to Ambleteuse near Boulogne (30 miles).

In all, twenty-one lines (780 miles) of 75mm diameter Pluto pipeline was laid, connecting pumping stations in England with receiving tanks in France. It is calculated that this procedure enabled 170,000 gallons of fuel to be pumped across to France by the end of the war. This saved lives, as it did not put the crews of tanker vessels at risk, was not vulnerable to the weather and could not be attacked by the enemy. Pluto guaranteed a reliable delivery of fuel in such quantities that the invasion army could pursue the retreating Germans relentlessly and without fear of running out of petrol. The technological requirements of Pluto in terms of pipeline itself and the pipelaying technique were cutting edge stuff for the time. It can also be argued that Pluto kick-started the technology of the whole offshore oil industry some sixty-three years ago. Swansea Museum has a piece of the Pluto pipeline in its Museum Stores at Landore.

St Illtyd's church, Ilston, Gower

I discovered the delightful Gower village of Ilston some years ago, when my wife, who is a calligrapher and heraldic artist, was commissioned to create an incumbents board to hang in the parish church of St Illtyd. An incumbents board records every vicar who has officiated there in the life of the church. The first entry reads 'Knights of St John 1341' and the last entry is the present vicar, Revd Canon David James Wilkinson, and is dated 1994. In between, there are 664 years of history and some thirty-seven vicars with an average tenure of approximately seventeen-and-a-half years each.

The parish of Ilston includes the villages of Parkmill, Lunnon and Ilston; it is linked with St Mary's Pennard and is served by the same vicar. To find the church, you leave Swansea by the Gower Road, cross the cattle grid on Fairwood Common and peel off onto the B4271. After a few miles, you turn off to Ilston and follow a meandering road down into the village, which is located beside a brook in a picturesquely wooded dell. Ilston contains a smattering of cottages and St Illtyd's is at the southern end of it and separated from the majority of the dwellings by the brook.

St Illtyd's church has its origins in a sixth-century monastic cell begun by early Celtic saints from Llantwit and Caldy. St Illtyd himself is thought to have been born in AD 475 and died in AD 537; his cousin was King Arthur, whom he served under. By 1128-29, St Illtyd's is being referred to in papal bulls as Llan Lldnt and Llancynwalon – the church of Ilston. The Knights of St John, who were given patronage, probably built the present tower, and the sixth-century monastic cell is in its base. The inside of the church is a delight. It is snug and cave-like, in the sense that there is an overwhelming feeling of security and safety. Finishes are primitive in the best sense of the word and you really feel that you are inside a special place. St Illtyd's has three bells, although only two (dating from 1716) are now rung. The other bell dates from the late fifteenth century and can be found immediately opposite the porch and entrance, which are

The snug cave-like interior of St Illtyd's church, looking up toward the chancel.

Victorian additions. This bell is cracked and was removed from the belfry in 1974; it was cast by the Bristol Medieval Bellfounding. A nice modern touch is the piece of contemporary stained glass by Paul Lucky of Swansea in the West Window, which dates from 1983. Outside, an old graveyard is full of headstones marbled with the bloom of lichens formed over many, many decades. Ilston church is described in *The Buildings of Wales* as a 'picturesque agglomeration'; you might say that also of Ilston village itself.

Stories in Stone – a Prehistoric Riverbed at Heathfield

Most of this book deals with 'history you can see' in the sense that it can easily be identified. However, sometimes history is so big you just do not recognise it as such and sometimes it is so small you will never notice it. Heathfield is a road that comes off the very steep road leading to Mount Pleasant and the Swansea Institute of Higher Education. It disappears behind the Windsor Lodge Hotel, revealing as it does so the exposed strata of the surrounding hillside.

A detail from the incumbents board made for the church by calligrapher Judith Porch.

You can see this exposed strata of rock at Heathfield; the bottom layer is a prehistoric river bed. The curved middle layer was once sand deposited as a sand bar.

To the average onlooker, it looks like many another rock strata left exposed when a road has been cut into some rising ground, but it has a story to tell. The rocks along Heathfield are sandstone, belonging to the group known as the Pennant Measures. Part of what is known as the Coal Measures in South Wales, these are basically sandstone interbedded with shale (mudrocks) and coal seams. They were once sediments deposited by large rivers that flowed across South Wales 320 million years ago in the Carboniferous period. At that time, Britain was part of an equatorial forest belt covered with abundant coal swamps. The position of all the world's continents was not fixed at this time and a map of the world would have looked very different from what we see today.

These sandstones with their interbedded coal seams are part of the South Wales coalfield which is roughly ninety-miles long on its east-west axis and roughly sixteen-miles wide. Such coal seams were worked all over the Swansea area, including Mount Pleasant, during the nineteenth century.

Numerous fossil can be seen in this rock used as a coping stone in a garden wall on Peniel Green Road. The biggest one is right in the centre of the photograph and is a coral in longitudinal section; the other circular ones are the same type of coral but seen from the top. They are over 300 million years old.

Most of the rocks exposed today are former sandstone quarries that would have been worked to provide building material and paving slabs to satisfy Swansea's rapid growth in the nineteenth century. You can still see locally quarried paving slabs on Constitution Hill and in the Maritime Quarter. Rosehill Quarry, further up Mount Pleasant, is another big exposure of the Pennant Measures. Quarrying began there in the 1840s, supplying building stone for local use; the Rosehill Quarry Group has since reclaimed it for local amenity use. Like the Half-Round Pond in the Enterprise Zone, it is considered one of Swansea's best kept secrets.

The photograph that accompanies this essay shows a curving mass of rock trapped between two other layers, as can be seen in the photograph. The surrounding layers are pointing upwards; these represent the general trend of the land surface when these rocks were formed as surface sediments. Sandwiched between these and inclined more to the horizontal is another layer of coarser material, known as a 'cross-bedding layer'. This middle layer was once sand deposited in the form of large bars in a river channel. The direction of inclination suggests that the river was flowing from left to right as you look at the photograph. The bottom layer of rock, the one pointing upward, is the ancient riverbed.

There is more evidence of prehistoric times in a garden wall on Peniel Green Road, in the form of a fossil that, along with many others, resides in a small boulder of carboniferous water-worn limestone used as a coping stone. The fossil looks deceptively like some form of long-extinct crustacean but is actually a longitudinal section through a single coral. This confirms the fact that the rock was once located in somewhat warmer climes than at present. Corals have a skeleton made up of a tube and each new floor in that skeleton represents growth; this species of coral is thought to be *Siphonophyllia*. This creature once lived in a tropical sea over 340 million years ago.

So, 100ft above the valley floor and in a side road just off Mount Pleasant you can see prehistoric evidence of an ancient riverbed that once existed 320million years ago. History is all around us, in garden walls, in the paving slabs beneath our feet and in the stone our houses are made of.

Swansea Infirmary

As you walk down St Helen's Road from the Guildhall end and cross Bryn-y-Mor Road near the Westbourne Hotel public house, you might easily miss a fragment of Swansea's social history. For on the corner of Phillips Parade and St Helen's Road stands the surviving pavilion of the former Swansea Infirmary.

The architect Alexander Graham built the infirmary for £14,000 between 1867 and 1869 in Pennant sandstone. At that time, the Infirmary stood on what were open fields on the edge of a steadily growing town with a population of around 50,000. In this period, medical care was not organised and was very often entirely in the gift of dispensaries operated on a voluntary basis. These dispensaries were essentially outpatient clinics for the poor and received their financial support from subscriptions raised from the rich and the not so rich at church or chapel. Although Swansea had its first voluntary infirmary as early as 1817, its work did not dovetail with the operation of the Poor Law. In short, if you could not afford to pay for medical advice and did not live within easy travelling distance (there were no horse-drawn trams until 1874) you either did without or self-dosed with whatever folk medicine was currently in fashion. It was in this vacuum that apothecaries and quack doctors – such as Baron Spolasco – existed to ply their wares to the poor and the gullible. By the 1850s, it was recognised that the town needed a bona fide infirmary capable of servicing a population, most of whom worked in heavy industry. Nevertheless, it was not to be built until the middle of the next decade. When it was, it came with the blessing of no less a person that Florence Nightingale (1820-1910), the nurse and heroine of the Crimean War. A letter from her, dated 18 November 1865, exists in the West Glamorgan Archives. In it she writes:

> Dear Sir,
> The account of your meeting about the new Swansea Infirmary, which you were kind enough to lend me has afforded me very real pleasure. Your enlightened Committee has rendered a real service to the course of humanity in adopting Mr Graham's beautiful plans. When completed you will have perhaps the finest and most perfect small hospital in the kingdom.

Although the infirmary was built to accommodate fifty beds, it was soon swamped with patients, a large percentage of whom were the victims of industrial accidents caused in and around the 600 furnaces that by then existed in the Lower Swansea Valley. This was at a time when the principal coppermasters in Swansea were the Vivian family, who had £800,000 in capital invested in that industry.

Another famous nursing heroine with a tenuous connection to Swansea Infirmary was Edith Cavell (1865-1915), who applied for a post at the infirmary in 1902. She achieved posthumous fame for her exploits during the First World War, when she aided soldiers to escape from

The surviving fragment of Swansea Infirmary as it looks in 2005.

occupied Belgium. In 1915, she was arrested by the Germans and summarily executed by firing squad, to general uproar.

The bulk of the hospital was demolished in the late 1980s, to be replaced with a sheltered housing scheme for the elderly; only a fragment of Alexander Graham's exotic essay in continental classicism remains.

Tennant Canal

As the traffic accelerates down Fabian Way towards Neath, it passes underneath a footbridge that allows pedestrians to cross this perennially busy stretch of dual carriageway from the Vale of Neath Road to Bevans Row on the other side. Alongside this road there is an unimpressive red brick building constructed in an irregular V-shape, which used to be the Vale of Neath Arms public house. This has now ceased to trade and the building is apparently back in private use. About 50 yards to the rear of this building can still be seen the remains of some of Swansea's

The Vale of Neath Arms public house in the 1930s, with the Tennant Canal meandering past it, heading towards Neath (Courtesy of West Glamorgan Archive Service).

This photograph was taken immediately behind the former Vale of Neath Arms public house. It shows the line of the Tennant Canal as it heads off towards Jersey Marine; the bridge over it is modern.

Georgian canal infrastructure. A large amount of dressed stone walling and a crude steel bridge signify that you have stumbled across the remains of what is commonly called the Tennant Canal, although according to the Neath and Tennant Canal Preservation Society it should be more accurately known as the Neath and Swansea Junction Canal. It was built between 1821 and 1824 in the reign of George IV by one George Tennant (1765-1832). Perhaps even more interesting is the fact that there used to be a stone bridge immediately in front of the Vale of Neath Arms which can still be seen in old photographs in the possession of the City and County Archives section at County Hall. The bridge spanned the Tennant Canal that then ran alongside the Vale of Neath Arms public house and roughly followed the line of today's Fabian Way in front of Bevans Row before disappearing behind the Prince of Wales Dock. Fabian Way did not exist then, being a product of the 1950s; before then, the whole area from the west side of the Prince of Wales Dock to the Inkerman Street area was comprised of railway sidings. There was only Fabian Street which ran from New Cut Bridge to Port Tennant Road and was hard up against the gable ends of the terraced housing at Miers Street, Inkerman Street, Balaclava Street and Sebastopol Street.

The origins of the Tennant Canal go back some 213 years, when one Edward Elton dug a canal from his colliery at Glan-y-wern to the River Neath in 1790. He did so in order to deliver coal to river barges that plied the river, as there was no link between the canal and the river in those days. Unfortunately, Edward Elton went bankrupt and died in 1810 and his canal fell into disuse. It was not until 1817 that George Tennant, the son of a Lancashire solicitor and owner of the Rhyddings Estate in Neath, took it over. His aim was to build a lock at the river, enabling barges to move from the river into the canal and vice versa. Although he could attract no financial support from local landowners, he nevertheless went ahead and completed the project by 1818. This canal was 4 miles in length and connected the rivers Tawe and Neath.

Tennant now turned his attention to connecting his canal to the Neath Canal. He did this by building a canal from Red Jacket through Neath Abbey, Cadoxton and Aberdulais to meet the Neath Canal. Once again, the headstrong and determined Tennant went ahead without the normal Act of Parliament needed, nor with the permission of the other landowners whose land the canal would cross. Work began in 1821 at the Red Jacket end. Not surprisingly, he was refused permission to cross land owned by Lewis Weston Dillwyn. Unfortunately for Tennant, Dillwyn held shares in the Neath Canal Company and was reluctant to do anything to help someone who might be a competitor. Tennant lost a year before arriving at a solution to the impasse by offering terms so favourable to Dillwyn and unfavourable to himself that they could not be refused. By 1823, Tennant's canal had reached the River Neath at Aberdulais; it was 8.5 miles long from Swansea to Aberdulais by the time it opened on 13 May 1824. Statistics reveal that 371 barges loaded with 5,930 tons of coal and timber used the new canal during the first seven weeks of its existence. By 1832, a passenger service was operating, carrying parcels, shop goods, corn and flour; it continued into the 1850s. Tennant's canal made a profit until 1895, despite stiff competition from the immediately adjacent Swansea and Neath Railway built in 1863. Nevertheless, the railways were the beginning of the end for canals and traffic fell steadily until it ceased completely in 1934, 110 years after it first started.

Trallwn Farm

If you drive out of central Swansea and into Bonymaen along Carmel Road, you pass the Halfway Inn, Lidl and The Range retail development. Keep going and you arrive at the top of Trallwn Road in Llasamlet. Keeping those retail units on your left and proceeding up Trallwn Road, you will soon see what looks like the stone outbuildings of a farm built up to the edge of the pavement. There is even a gated entrance leading to what looks exactly like a farmyard and a whitewashed farmhouse set back from the road. As one invariably passes all this at speed, it simply does not register as a farmhouse because the context is all wrong. Modern Llansamlet was mostly built as a residential suburb in the 1960s and later, so how would an old farmhouse get there? But No. 77 Trallwn Road is a farmhouse and was for many years known as Trallwn Farm. Indeed, some kind of housing or cottages belonging to a farm have been on that spot for nearly 200 years, according to old maps of the district.

Of course, the story of Trallwn Farm is the story of Llansamlet's fortunes in the nineteenth century. Situated three miles north-east of the city centre, Llansamlet is on the eastern side of the Lower Swansea Valley. In the mid-eighteenth century it was agricultural land dotted with many

Number 77 Trallwn Road. There have been farm buildings on this site since the 1830s.

99

small farms all linked by country lanes. However, what Llansamlet also had was coal reserves, most of which could be worked both easily and inexpensively. This was being done as early as the 1700s. By the middle of the nineteenth century, collieries in Llansamlet were exporting 70,000 tons of coal a year. Later that same century, the smelting of copper and zinc began in earnest, industries which lasted into the second half of the twentieth century. In the mid-1800s, Llansamlet was also one of the few Welsh-speaking parishes left. Unfortunately, it was also 'a treeless, shrubless waste' according to the contemporary physician and polymath Dr Thomas Williams. By the mid-century and the height of the copper industry there were something like 300 furnace chimneys in the Lower Swansea Valley. The ponds of Llansamlet were devoid of pond life and grazing animals died of mysterious diseases in fields polluted by copper smoke and worse.

An undated photograph of Thomas Thomas.

It is against this background that we must see Trallwn Farm. The earliest maps I have seen of Trallwn date from 1830, when it was called Trallwyn and was comprised of hardly more than half a dozen cottages and farms. Trallwn Road seems to have existed then but was probably nothing more than a track. The next earliest map I consulted was the 1881 Ordnance Survey map, which showed that Trallwyn was basically a small village comprised of approximately fifty terraced cottages clustered in small groups astride a main road. The Halfway Inn can be seen, although the one we see now was built in 1928. Number 77 Trallwn Road, as we now know it, had not yet been built; instead, a short terrace of three cottages stood on the site, backing onto large fields running down to the valley floor. The heart of Trallwyn in 1881 was a nucleus of cottages astride a road and intersected by two lanes which can still be seen in much altered form today. The extent of the village then is easily defined and went from the house now known as No. 52 at the Bonymaen end to No. 116 at the Bethel Road end.

Even by 1881, there were numerous pits both in use and already disused. There was a quarry to the rear of where No. 82 is today on land still vacant. In addition to pits and quarries, there was

No. 55/6.

BRITON FERRY ESTATE.

No. **3388**

26 NOV 1930

Received of Mr. Thomas Thomas

the sum of _____ Sixteen Pounds,

_____ fifteen Shillings, and _____ Pence,

being Two Quarters of a Year's Rent, due the 29th September, 1930, to the

Trustees for The Right Honourable The EARL OF JERSEY,

for Fields Houses, Lands, and Premises at, or known as

Llwyn Crwn Trallwng Farm

situate in the Parish or Hamlet of **LLANSAMLET.**

Rent ... ... £ 16 : 15 :

Income Tax allowed ... - : - : -

Net Amount received £ 16 : 13 : -

J B Williams

A rent receipt from the Briton Ferry Estate made out to the Llwyn Crwn Trallwn Farm.

BARR'S COURT CIDER WORKS,

'Phone : Hereford 2251.
Telegrams : "Boulton, Hereford."

AUG 1932

Hereford,.............

Mr T Thomas.

ᶜᵒ **J. BOULTON & SONS, Ltd.**

. **CIDER & PERRY MAKERS.**

All Casks not returned within N I N E M O N T H S to be paid for.

*Bankers—National Provincial
and Union Bank of England, Hereford Branch.*

Ledger Folio...............................

D . T . 121 .

P L E A S E   N O T E .— *All Orders and Remittances by Postal Order or Cheque
must be sent direct to the Firm at Hereford and not to agents or travellers.*

NO RECEIPT VALID UNLESS ON OWN PRINTED RECEIPT FORMS.

1932.

May	11	To Cider		16	6

Folio D.T. 121

3261

HEREFORD, 28 . 9 . 193

Rec'd *from* Mr J Thomas

£   s.   d.   C. 2/4   D.   R.

— 14 7

FOR J. BOULTON & SONS, LTD.

p.p.

Number Casks not ret'd   1 No.   8865 . £1—0—0
Number Cases not ret'd   No.

With Compliments.

If any error found, please return at once to be corrected.

**PLEASE NOTE.—All Remittances and Orders should be sent direct to
Cider Works, Hereford.**

One of numerous receipts still in the possession of Ken Hughes that testify to his grandfather's taste for cider.

also a deadly array of industrial enterprises on the valley floor, all within a mile or so of where the village lay. These were the Swansea Chemical Works, Swansea Vale Spelter, Villiers Spelter Works, Swansea Smelter Works and the Llansamlet Spelter Works. But in 1881 the creation of No. 77 Trallwn Road was still nineteen years in the future. It was built in 1900 by Thomas Thomas, grandfather of current owner Ken Hughes. Thomas started renting Trallwn Farm from the Earl of Jersey, who owned most of the land in Llansamlet in 1900, and demolished the three cottages on it to make room for the present building. Ken Hughes still has receipts from the Briton Ferry Estate dating from the 1930s, showing Thomas Thomas paying £16 15s for half a year's rent to the 'Trustees for The Right Honourable The Earl of Jersey' for fields known as 'Llwyn Crwn Trallwng Farm'. The extent of Trallwn Farm (in modern terms) was bounded by the recreation fields adjacent to the Halfway Inn and went as far to the west as Llwyn Crwn Road and as far north as Bethel Chapel on Bethel Road. Trallwn Road formed the natural eastern boundary to the farm.

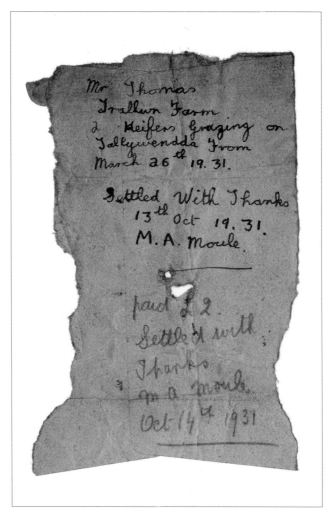

A receipt made out on a scrap of paper from a farmer called M.A.Moule for allowing Thomas Thomas to graze two heifers on an adjacent farm.

Family legend has it that Thomas Thomas hauled the stone he needed for his new farmhouse from Briton Ferry by handcart. He was by all accounts a bit of a character; he branded all his agricultural equipment with two Ts and was a Tory voter through and through. So much so that he flew the Tory flag from a flagpole in the yard and made a point of drinking at the Halfway Inn which, due to political allegiance, enjoyed a local reputation as 'little Moscow'. Thomas Thomas did not confine his tippling to the local inn; he also bought cider by the cask from J. Boulton & Sons Ltd of Hereford. Numerous receipts dating from the early 1930s and still in the possession of Ken Hughes testify to Thomas Thomas's thirst for cider. He used to pay 14s 2d a cask, which roughly converts into present money as nearly 75p. Ken Hughes has another receipt dating from October 1931 and written on the back of what must have been an old envelope. A farmer called M.A. Moule made it out to the value of £2 for 'Mr Thomas, Trallwng Farm, 2 Heifers Grazing on Tallywendda Farm from March 26th 1931. Settled with thanks 13th October 1931'. Tallywendda Farm was located about a mile to the south of Trallwn Farm and more towards Swansea. Thomas Thomas may have liked his cider but it nicely demonstrates how businesslike he was, as he kept this receipt, in reality nothing more than a scrap of brown paper, on a spike along with hundreds of others still in the possession of his grandson Ken. There are two such spikes, each about 305mm long, attached to a small timber block on which Thomas Thomas spiked every receipt he ever got. They constitute a snapshot of agricultural life in the Lower Swansea Valley during the period 1917-60. The bulk of the receipts are from local firms for goods or services purchased but every now and then there are mysterious things like receipts for being ferried home by ambulance! In those pre-National Health Service days I suppose you were liable for things like that. Why Thomas Thomas needed an ambulance is not recorded, we can only speculate as to whether it was due to overindulgence at the Halfway Inn or an agricultural accident.

Agricultural workers on Trallwn Farm in the 1930s or '40s. The two haybarns stood roughly where No. 67 Trallwn Road is today.

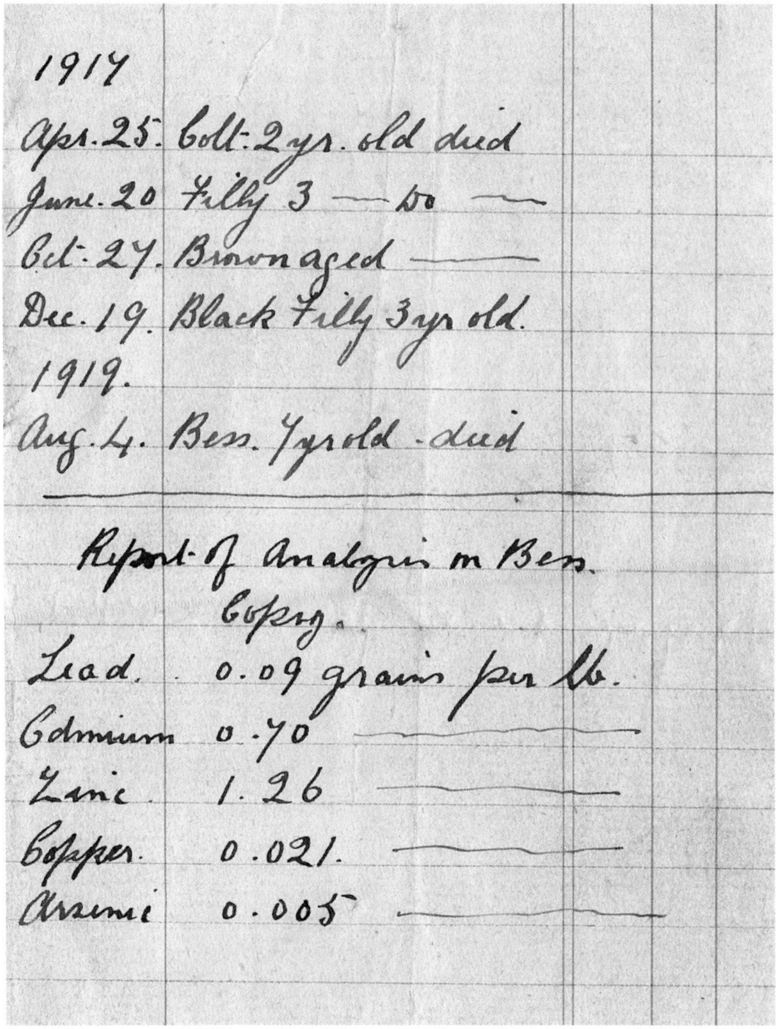

1917

Apr. 25. Colt. 2 yr. old died

June. 20 Filly 3 — do —

Oct. 27. Brown aged —

Dec. 19. Black Filly 3 yr old.

1919.

Aug. 4. Bess. 7 yr old - died

Report of Analysis on Bess.

Copry.

Lead . 0.09 grains per lb.

Cadmium 0.70 —

Zinc . 1.26 —

Copper. 0.021. —

Arsenic 0.005 —

In the early twentieth century, Thomas Thomas kept a notebook that recorded the death of horses on his farm. A seven-year-old horse called Bess died on 4 August 1919 and the book contains a breakdown of the chemicals found in her upon analysis.

In the late 1930s, with war seemingly imminent, the War Department requisitioned land belonging to Trallwn Farm for the creation of a magazine or ammunition dump. Ken Hughes thinks that this 'took the heart out of the farm'. The magazine was used to store ammunition in a concrete bunker that was visible until quite recently. You can see the rough dimensions of the magazine still, as the road called Lon Enfys encompasses its below-ground location. The magazine is thought to be still down there and is defined as a green area within the boundaries of the Lon Enfys Road housing development. The war came to Trallwn Farm one night in 1941, when a stick of bombs fell across the farm and fields. Ken Hughes, who has lived at Trallwn Farm all his life, can remember as a boy filling in those craters with rubble after the war. At the war's end, the War Department offered to sell the land containing the magazine back to

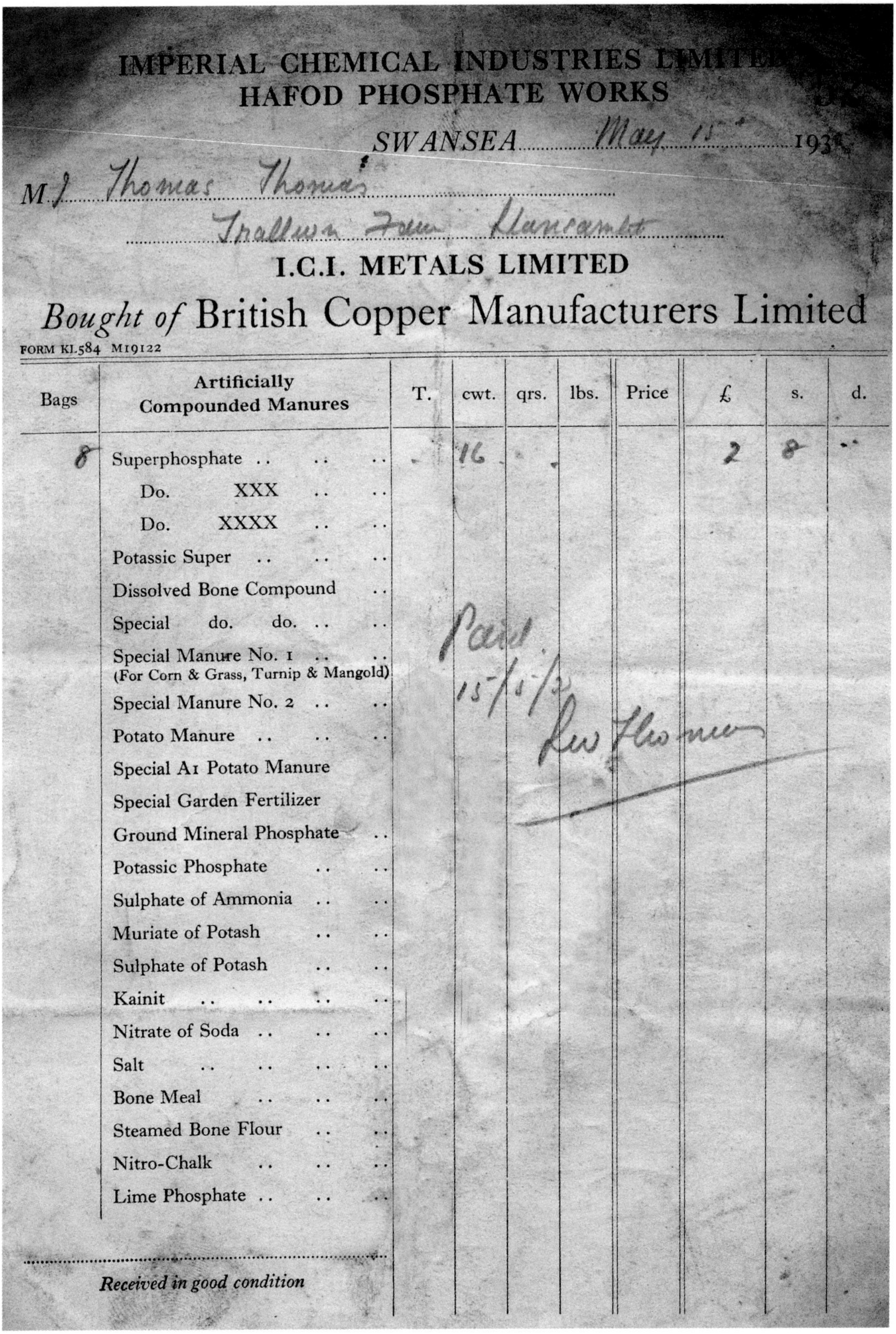

IMPERIAL CHEMICAL INDUSTRIES LIMITED
HAFOD PHOSPHATE WORKS
SWANSEA...........May 15......193

M. *Thomas Thomas*

Trallwn Farm Llansamlet

I.C.I. METALS LIMITED
Bought of British Copper Manufacturers Limited

FORM KL.584 MI9122

Bags	Artificially Compounded Manures	T.	cwt.	qrs.	lbs.	Price	£	s.	d.
8	Superphosphate		16				2	8	..
	Do. XXX								
	Do. XXXX								
	Potassic Super								
	Dissolved Bone Compound ..								
	Special do. do.								
	Special Manure No. 1								
	(For Corn & Grass, Turnip & Mangold)								
	Special Manure No. 2								
	Potato Manure								
	Special A1 Potato Manure								
	Special Garden Fertilizer								
	Ground Mineral Phosphate ..								
	Potassic Phosphate								
	Sulphate of Ammonia								
	Muriate of Potash								
	Sulphate of Potash								
	Kainit								
	Nitrate of Soda								
	Salt								
	Bone Meal								
	Steamed Bone Flour								
	Nitro-Chalk								
	Lime Phosphate								

Paid
15/5/3
Rev Thomas

Received in good condition

Above: *Hay being gathered in at Trallwn Farm in the 1930s or '40s, a sight never to be seen again.*

Opposite: *This receipt shows Thomas Thomas buying 16cwt of superphosphate fertiliser with which to manure his land.*

the family but they could not afford to pay the new asking price and it was sold at auction to a local builder.

In its day, Trallwn Farm was used to grow root crops and hay at its southern end nearest the Halfway Inn and the rest was used for grazing. Indeed, Ken Hughes can remember his father growing crops all the way down to the Swansea Vale works. The works operated under that name between 1876 and 1924, then carried on as the National Smelting Co. Ltd until 1964. In its day, it supplied all the local needs of the town. Like many of the other metallurgical concerns that operated near the farm, it produced spelter, or zinc, whose chief use is in galvanising. Unlike the unsuccessful farmers in the famous Llansamlet copper smoke trials of the early 1830s, Thomas Thomas succeeded in proving that pollution from the National Smelting Co. Ltd was polluting his land. He did this just after the war by means of sheets of 2ft square panes of wired glass set within a steel frame being left out in the fields and exposed to the prevailing wind. When sent away for analysis, they showed the characteristic clouding that demonstrated the presence of airborne pollution. Even more poignantly, there survives a page from a notebook belonging to Thomas Thomas dating from 1917 in which he records the death of horses from pollution. Trallwn Farm's land was presumably kept usable by means of extensive manuring; a receipt dated 1931 still in the possession of Ken Hughes shows Thomas Thomas buying 16cwt of superphosphates from what was then ICI. It had originally been the Vivians Hafod works up until 1924 when the Hafod and Morfa works were amalgamated to form British Copper Manufacturers. They were in turn taken over by Imperial Chemical Industries in 1926. The invoice contains a menu of ICI products sold from its Hafod Phosphate Works, which included potato manure, salt, special manure for corn and grass, turnip and mangold, and special garden fertiliser. It is ironic that this firm, along with many others, had done so much to pollute the Lower Swansea Valley in the nineteenth century, ended up selling manure products to local farmers for agricultural purposes. There is a nice cycle of history at work there.

Ken's father, William Phillip Hughes, took over Trallwn Farm from Thomas Thomas and ran it until Thomas' other son, Wyn, took over from him in turn. Trallwn Farm functioned as a farm until as late as 1958/59, when the remaining fields were sold to the council as they had ceased to be viable for farming. In the early 1960s, Ken's mother was offered the house, outbuildings and two acres, which she bought. The last animal slaughtered on the farm was a pig called Nookey-nook in the early 1960s. It was the runt of a litter that Ken's mother had kept and, according to Ken's wife Elaine, 'it followed people around like a dog'. Ken remembers that when his father had pigs slaughtered he would wrap them in linen cloth and hang them from hooks embedded in the ceiling of the large downstairs room. Coming in from work, he would peel back the cloth and carve himself a few rashers of bacon and cook them on the open fire that still exists. There was also a long old-fashioned farmhouse kitchen table in that room where Ken Hughes still remembers eating meals of giblet soup, liver and lights and pig's head.

Trallwn Farm is an important reminder of a Llansamlet that has long vanished. A Llansamlet comprised of farms, small collieries and quarries, where people eked out a living from what they could grow or gouge out of the land. Trallwn Farm is 'history you can see' personified and is easily missed among the large housing estate that 'Trallwyn' has become.

Vincent Street School

Since the 1950s, school architecture seems to have taken most of its cues from office block design more than anywhere else. It is probably the numbers of pupils to be accommodated that drives the design of schools, with the consequence that they often resemble nothing more than a sequence of glazed boxes set unimaginatively in the landscape. However, the requirement to accommodate sheer numbers can be handled positively, as our inheritance of Victorian Board schools demonstrates. In the late nineteenth century, two things drove the design of schools. The first was the advent of the Elementary Education Act of 1870, which required universal education for all children. This triggered an increase in the number of new schools needed. Secondly, the populations of towns and cities were growing rapidly so new and bigger schools were needed on a scale never before known. This translated into the tactic of separating the sexes, with girls on the ground floor, boys on an upper floor and the removal of infants to a separate building. Gone were the days of one large schoolroom separated down the middle with boys on one side and girls on the other and mixed ages and abilities all pitched in together.

In the earlier part of the nineteenth century, the education of children was left to the initiative of concerned townspeople and, in Swansea, the coppermasters. Pascoe St Leger Grenfell established Swansea's first works school as long ago as 1806; it was extended in 1839 and 1850. J.H. Vivian built another school in 1846 that can still be seen today on Vivian Street in the Hafod, although these days it is a community centre rather than a school. The teachers were paid from deductions in the wages of employees.

By the end of the nineteenth century, the Board schools were nearly always built in Gothic style, made from stone and looking quite unlike today's flimsy-looking essays in concrete and glass.

My favourite Swansea Board school is in Vincent Street and is now called St Helen's Primary School. It was opened two years after Queen Victoria died, on 14 July 1903, and the architect was G.E.T. Laurence of London. Laurence specialised in schools, having trained in the office of the foremost Board school architect, E.R.Robson, who was also based in London. His 1874 book *School Architecture* was highly influential and advocated three-storey buildings with the sexes divided as mentioned earlier. Although Vincent Street is not a three-storey affair, it is a model of good design practice especially in the wake of the Dunblane tragedy. Vincent Street School is domestically scaled and built around a playground that basically functions as a village square. An outer ring of school buildings and bicycle sheds has been wrapped around it in a U-shape to create a secure environment for children to play in. This design prevents intruders in a way that is both civilised and natural. The playground is overlooked on three sides by numerous windows, ostensibly to supply light to classrooms, corridors and offices, but they also enable staff to monitor the playground, which cannot really be seen from the street as it is shielded by the mass of the school's buildings. As a result, no one can really spy on the children without drawing attention to themselves. A big iron school gate is the final and most basic measure to control access; other than that, it is the architecture of the school that does the job.

G.E.T. Laurence also built Manselton Primary School in Manor Road, Manselton in 1900-1902. He also designed St Thomas Primary School on Windmill Street in 1897. A red brick four-storey structure for 1,200 pupils, it is the most prominent structure in St Thomas and can still be seen from Quay Parade. Both designs were driven by the need to stack classrooms and accommodate large numbers of pupils on confined sites. Most eye-catching of all is Laurence's Teacher Training College in Pant-Y-Celyn Road, Townhill. Built in 1911 and executed in a distinctive Elizabethan style, it is now part of the Swansea Institute of Higher Education.

A sketch of Vincent Street School. The design of the school provides a secure environment in a civilised and natural way.

This is a rubbing taken from the top of a steel die used to stamp blocks of highly toxic black oxide of cobalt at the Vivians' nickel and cobalt works that used to be situated near the Hafod.

Vivian & Co. Steel Die

Sometimes you stumble across history in Swansea and sometimes it stumbles across you. An instance of the latter occurred a year or so ago after writing my local history column for the *Swansea Leader.* A Mr Lethaby sent me an email very kindly offering to donate what he described as a heavy metal stamp. It turned out to be the size of a soup plate, roughly 5in (125mm) thick and extremely heavy. Its top surface was inscribed and, after producing a rubbing using paper and a wax crayon, the words 'Black Oxide of Cobalt, Manufactured by H.H. Vivian & Co, Nickel & Cobalt Works, Swansea, England' were revealed. It turned out to be a steel die used in a steam-powered press to compact blocks of cobalt oxide during the period 1883-1895. Cobalt oxide was a toxic by-product of the nickel-cobalt smelting process and was mainly used for imparting a blue colour to glass and for colouring pottery glazes. Although the die is marked as having been manufactured by H.H. Vivian and Co., the actual company that manufactured it was a personal enterprise of Henry Hussey Vivian rather than a branch of the main firm. It was called the Hafod Isha Nickel Works and was founded in 1855 by H.H. Vivian in collaboration with his father J.H. Vivian. It was built to refine nickel and cobalt from refined ores and concentrates imported from Canada. Henry Vivian visited Canada and bought his own mines there. The Hafod Isha works could be found alongside the river and stretched from Maliphant Street to Jersey Street (both of which can be seen today) and was separated from them by railway lines and the Swansea Canal. The company was operated under that title until shortly after 1895, when it was sold off to the Anglo-French Nickel Co. Ltd. The works produced nickel, cobalt oxide in powder form and other contaminants. The smelting process would have produced cobalt oxide as a powder and this would have been compressed into blocks for ease of handling. Hence the need for a steel die that could also mark the product with the maker's name.

The toxicity of cobalt smelting was understood as long ago as medieval times and until the twentieth century the only measure taken to mitigate this was to allow the fumes to escape up a tall chimney and allow the wind to disperse them. This was the tactic of all Swansea's smelting works, whether copper or otherwise, with the result that a powerfully toxic cocktail of copper smoke was produced that blighted the landscape, the grazing animals and the lives of all humans under its pall. For all the much-vaunted scientific and technical inventiveness of the Victorians, they somehow never got around to doing toxicological studies of this copper smoke. Had they done so, they would have found that such smoke contained, besides nickel cobalt fumes, a wide range of heavy metals and acids. Had the die been a block of cobalt oxide instead, it would have been a highly toxic substance, especially if it had started to revert to its original powdered form.

Mr Lethaby's innocuous steel die, originally used as a doorstop, is a very tangible reminder of Swansea's metal industries and everything that went with them. It is destined to find a home in one of the collections of the new Maritime and Industrial Museum.

War Damage

When we want to see what Swansea looked like when it was bombed for three consecutive nights in February 1941, we usually just reach for the history books. Little do we realise that the scars of the Three Nights' Blitz can still be seen in the fabric of the modern city. Most of the town centre was levelled when between sixty and seventy aircraft of the German Third Air Fleet flying from occupied France dropped an estimated 800 high-explosive bombs and 30,000 incendiaries on Swansea.

However, not all of the centre was destroyed: the former Central police station occupying its triangular site flanked by Orchard Street on one side and Alexandra Road on the other survived. It was built between 1912 and 1913 by Ernest E. Morgan (1881-54), who was the Borough Architect of Swansea from 1913-43. Constructed in red brick and Portland stone, it is a tangible reminder of the Three Nights' Blitz. If you look carefully at the Orchard Street elevation of the building, you will see that it is pockmarked with shrapnel damage from those three devastating nights. An eyewitness statement given by a police officer recorded that the 'only buildings left standing seemed to be the Central Police Station and the Mount Pleasant church. Apart from that, most of the area was completely devastated, streets were piled up with wreckage, buildings had collapsed across the road so that roads themselves were blocked'.

The human cost included 230 killed, 409 injured and 7,000 made homeless out of a population of 167,000. The Three Nights' Blitz actually lasted thirteen hours and forty-eight minutes in total.

Shrapnel damage from bombs dropped during the Three Nights' Blitz is still visible on the Orchard Street elevation of the former Central Police Station.

Weaver & Company Ltd Building

The Weaver & Company Ltd building dominated Swansea's dockland skyline for eighty-seven years between 1897 and 1984 and occupies a place in the history of British architecture. For Weaver's was the first building constructed using reinforced concrete in Swansea and indeed one of the first in the world. The Frenchman François Hennebique (1842–1921) devised a method of construction using reinforced concrete in the 1870s. Reinforced concrete contains metal bars and it is their placing and dimensions that give the material its unique structural properties. By 1892, Hennebique had built his first reinforced floor slabs and also patented a building system using reinforced structural beams. By 1902, he had built 7,206 bridges, factories, municipal buildings and water towers using this material. Weaver's was a vast grain mill that could produce 900 bags of brown bread flour an hour and had a reservoir containing 20,000 gallons of water on its roof. Surviving photographs show a narrow rectangular block of distinctly fortress-like appearance looming over the half-tide basin of the North Dock, which inevitably became

The austere bulk of the Weaver & Company Ltd building as it looked in dereliction during the 1970s.

known as Weaver's Basin. The architect was H.C. Portsmouth and the contractors were the local firm of Thomas, Watkins and Jenkins; the contract started on 20 October 1897 and was completed on 1 August 1898.

The Weaver's building was a real product of its age; the 1890s were a decade whose inventions would change the world forever. Henry Ford created the Model T Ford in 1896, André and Edouard Michelin produced the first pneumatic tyre and Marconi made the first wireless transmissions over distances of 2,400 metres. In addition, Roentgen discovered X-rays, Ferdinand Braun created the first cathode-ray tube and William Kellogg invented cornflakes.

Weaver's went into decline as white bread from abroad became more popular in the 1920s. Nevertheless, surviving maps and plans show that the North Dock was filled in long before Weaver's Basin closed. Weaver's eventually closed in 1963 and was demolished in 1984. One of its reinforced concrete columns was preserved and can still be seen on the riverside walkway near New Cut Bridge.

White Rock Archaeological Park

At any time up until its demolition in the 1960s, the White Rock site was arguably of what we now call world heritage status. The demolition of the surviving above-ground features teaches us a salutary lesson about how our relationship with history is not a constant one; it changes with circumstances. One moment we respect history and what it can teach us; the next it is merely an unpleasant reminder of a past we want to banish. The timescales involved can often be short. The surviving works were bulldozed in 1965 and the White Rock Archaeological Park created in the 1980s. Surviving photographs of the site in the 1960s show a wealth of ruined buildings dating from the eighteenth, nineteenth and twentieth centuries. It was a veritable open-air museum of Swansea's industrial heritage, although a dangerous one in terms of pollution and unsafe structures, due to the derelict nature of the site.

White Rock had sustained (or endured) nearly two centuries of continuous industrialisation starting in 1737 and not really ending until 1929, when they were still making sheet and pipe there. Unlike the other major copperworks owned by the Vivian and Grenfell families, who came from Cornwall, White Rock was founded by Bristol interests. We are so used to thinking of Swansea as Copperopolis, we forget that Bristol was the centre of the British copper industry in the late seventeenth and early eighteenth centuries. White Rock stayed a copperworks until 1871, when it became a lead and silver works owned by Williams, Foster and Co. From 1871 to 1874, they operated it in partnership with Vivian & Sons but after 1874 the Vivians operated it alone until 1924. For two years until 1926 it was part of British Copper Manufacturers, which was in turn taken over by ICI.

The legacy of all that industrialisation was the White Rock tip that was 33 hectares in size. It was comprised of 183,000 tons of copper waste and cost £129,210 to clear in 1967-8. This material was not taken away and simply dumped on someone else's doorstep. Instead it was used to raise the level of land previously occupied by the Worcester and Upper Forest tinplate works on what we now call the Enterprise Park. Morganite Carbon was built on it near Morriston.

If you look at White Rock now, it superficially appears denuded of all its history and the site is frequently riven with the tyre marks of off-road bikers. Yet 155 years ago White Rock was covered with buildings and the transportation network needed to sustain a copperworks. For example, you can still see a river dock, one of fourteen that used to be on the river, where ore-carrying vessels could tie up and unload. On an 1876 Ordnance Survey map, you can see the whole area below the dock designated as White Rock Quay, paved most probably with home-made slag blocks and dotted with cast-iron mooring posts. The site seems to undulate and exist on a number of levels.

All that remains of Francois Hennebique's vast grain mill created for Weaver & Company Ltd is this column, which lies in repose on the riverbank near New Cut Bridge. It was a pioneering piece of industrial architecture made from reinforced concrete.

This is probably because they tipped onto the site and then built upon the compacted remains. Along the river's edge, there appears to be a low-level buttressed wall; this can be seen on numerous old photographs of the site and is a stone-faced edge to a plateau created by previous slag tipping. To the very back of the site, near the Pentre-Chwyth Road, can still be seen the eighteenth-century remains of what was called the Great Workhouse in its day. This was not a workhouse in the sense the poor were sent there, rather it was the smelting-hall of the White Rock works and has been estimated at 340ft long by 40ft wide. It would have housed a single row of furnaces running its full length. Behind this, the ground has been raised to accommodate one of the White Rock site's more fascinating features, a canal hidden in a tunnel which was buried in order to minimise its intrusion into the works. Three miles long, John Smith's Llansamlet Canal replaced Chauncey Townsend's wagonway of the 1750s; it was constructed in 1783-4 in order to deliver coal from Smith's colliery at Llansamlet to the river. Its path took it from Gwernllwynchwyth House, through Llansamlet, the Enterprise Park and past the Addis works, ending up at a terminus below All Saints church at Kilvey. You can still see an entrance to Smith's subterranean canal as you walk towards Foxhole, although it is very much hidden by undergrowth and you have to look for it. Perhaps the most amazing survivor of the White Rock site is a tiny stone aqueduct that carries a stream running off Kilvey over the tunnel containing Smith's canal and off down a watercourse into the River Tawe. Again, this feature is well hidden by undergrowth but you can find it, especially if you use the footbridge over the cyclepath that runs along the river.

White Rock was Swansea's third oldest copperworks and has some of the most interesting features still to be seen; there is surely even more awaiting excavation.

The White Rock Archaeological Park in the mid-1960s, in total dereliction.

The White Rock Archaeological Park in 2004. The chimneys of the engine house for the Hafod copperworks can be seen in the centre. The restored river dock in the foreground is one of fourteen that used to be on the river at which vessels could tie up and unload copper ore.

An entrance to Smith's canal, constructed between 1783 and 1784 and still visible today through the undergrowth.

A stone aqueduct carries a stream running off Kilvey Hill over the top of Smith's canal, which is buried beneath, and onto a watercourse.

Whitford Point Lighthouse

The light from Whitford Point lighthouse has not blinked across the Burry Estuary since 1926, when the light from its 44ft high tower could be seen for 7 miles. Situated 1 mile from the North Gower coast, the shell of Britain's only wave-washed cast-iron lighthouse is only accessible for a few hours each day at low tide, which is perhaps just as well given that the Burry Estuary was used as a gunnery range during the Second World War. Although the Whiteford Sands have been regularly swept for unexploded ordnance, the odd shell has turned up over the years.

The present lighthouse is the second built on the Whitford Sker; the first was of timber construction and was built in 1854. John Paisley Luckraft, the Harbour Master at Llanelli, designed it and it became operational in 1855. Within ten years, it had been severely damaged by a mixture of devastating storms and collisions with vessels and a new one was needed. The Llanelli Harbour Commissioners decided in 1865 that they needed to mark the approach channel to the port with a new lighthouse. They also decided to site this one 300 yards south of the old one and the task of designing it was given to John Bowen, a local engineer at the Llanelli copperworks. Llanelli, like Swansea at this time, was a centre for the copper industry in Wales, which explains how copper came to be used in the glazing bars and roofing to the lighthouse. Bowen's design called for a structure 22ft (6.71m) in diameter at its base, tapering gradually to a lantern with a diameter of 11ft 6in (3.5m). The structure of the lighthouse was made from seven large cast-iron rings to which are bolted thick plates that use external flanges as opposed to internal ones. This was done presumably to facilitate ease of replacement, should damage to any of the plates occur. The resultant finish, therefore, is not smooth as with a conventional lighthouse but looks as if it has grown organically like some giant species of coral. As if in counterpoint to the stark massiveness of the tower, the balusters and brackets that support the balcony around the lantern were executed in a flimsy-looking but decorative gothic style. At high tide, the lighthouse stands in 20ft of water with access to it gained by means of an external ladder now long-since removed. This and the Spartan living accommodation aboard leads one to conclude that the lighthouse was not inhabited and was maintained by someone walking out over the sand and the mud every day. The Whitford Point lighthouse was still in use by 1914 but not by 1933. The dereliction of the last seventy-two years has stripped the lantern of all its glass, roof and the flooring to the balcony, leaving the lighthouse like the carapace of some long-dead crustacean picked clean by the seagulls and the weather. An uninhabitable cast-iron shell now, it was offered for sale for £1 and plans to use it for a solar-powered laser display as part of the Millennium Coastal Park came to nothing because of the expense.

The Whitford Point lighthouse is an enduring example of Victorian cast-iron engineering and stands forlornly out on the sands, an archaic relic of another age. It is readily visible from Pembrey and Burry Port and is no longer for sale.

Whitford Point lighthouse stands on the north coast of Gower and is the only cast-iron wave-washed tower in British waters. It is an enduring example of Victorian engineering and stands in 20ft (6.096m) of water at high tide each day. (Graham Bell).

two

History you can see in a street name

TAPLOW TERRACE

History can reside in something as everyday as a street name and this section offers a brief explanation of the origin of some of the street names of Swansea and district.

Adelaide Street is in Swansea's Maritime Quarter conservation area. When you next walk down the street, spare a thought for the origins of the street name. You first start to see Adelaide Street on street plans of Swansea dating from the 1830s. The person referred to was none other than William IV's wife, Queen Adelaide. She was born Adelhied Luise Therese Caroline Amalie on 13 August 1792 at Meiningen and her mother was Louise Hohenlohe-Langenburg. Adelhied is German for 'noble woman' and Adelaide took a keen interest in the charitable poor, the funding of schools, church buildings and the promotion of Christian knowledge. Despite a twenty-seven-year difference in their ages, she married William IV (1765-1837) on 7 November 1818 at Kew Palace in Richmond, Surrey. The third son of George III, he ascended to the throne of England on 26 June 1830 upon the death of his brother George IV (1762-1830) and was crowned at Westminster Abbey in London. There were two children of their marriage but both died in early infancy while four others were stillborn. The Australian city of Adelaide was named after William IV's consort in July 1836, when the colony was proclaimed; it is the only Australian capital named after a woman. Despite William IV fathering no less than ten illegitimate children by the actress Mrs Dorothy Jordan, Queen Adelaide was regarded as a model of respectability and is credited with restoring the credibility of the monarchy at a time when the rest of Europe were replacing their monarchs via revolution. King William IV died at Windsor Castle on 20 June 1837 and was succeeded in turn by his brother's daughter Victoria (1818-1901). Queen Adelaide died on 2 December 1849 and was buried in St George's chapel, Windsor.

Bath Lane in the city centre does not owe its name to the manufacture of any kind of household furniture but to one of Swansea's biggest shipowning families in the Victorian period. Henry Bath and his son were Quakers originating from Falmouth, who moved to Swansea in 1816. Henry Bath (1776-1864) was the first of the family to do so and leased a copper ore yard in what we now call Bath Lane from the Corporation in 1822 and held monthly samplings for market there. He also went into partnership with R.J Nevill to found the Landore copperworks in 1827, which lasted until 1837. Certain copper manufacturers began to develop interests in copper refineries nearer to the source of all the copper in South America. To this end, Henry Bath sent his sons Henry, James and Edward to Chile to oversee smelting operations there in the 1840s. Henry Bath must have been an astute man of business, as by 1838 he was living in Cambrian Place, in what was very much the better end of town. The Bath ships, which numbered thirty at one time, were usually built at Bideford in North Devon and were named after the letters of the Greek alphabet: *Alpha, Beta, Gamma, Zeta* and so on. When the sea wall was being built in the Maritime Quarter during the 1980s, it was decided to commemorate these vessels by carving their names into it. They can still be seen today. Bath was also a fan of the contemporary American writer James Fennimore Cooper (1789-1851), who wrote about the early frontier and the Native American Indians. So much so that he also named some of his ships after characters from those novels, such as *Uncas*, *Mohican* and *Deerslayer*. Bath's vessels were the nautical equivalent of the transcontinental heavy goods vehicles of today. They were the Cape Horners of legend, barques that would go out loaded with Welsh coal or patent fuel and come back laden with the even heavier South American copper ore. Their route took them around the fearsome Cape Horn and then up the west coast of South America, an arduous voyage that gave both crew and vessel a terrific pounding. The Baths could trace their family history all the way back to 1217 and Sir Walter de Bath, who was Sheriff of Devon. The family motto was the suitably pious Victorian one of 'He conquers who endures'. By 1888, the Baths had diversified into ship breaking and paid £16,000 for Brunel's *Great Eastern* in order to turn it into scrap. It took two years to dismantle it on the beach at Birkenhead. Also in 1888, the last of Henry Bath's sons died; however, the firm remained in private hands until the early 1970s, when it was bought by the British Bank of Commerce. It has changed hands many times since and is now involved in the buying and selling of steel. Nevertheless, 182 years after the Baths first came to Swansea, you can still find a Bath Lane in the Maritime Quarter's conservation area and a website devoted to the company's current dealings.

Burrows Place and **East Burrows Road** can be found in the Maritime Quarter. How often does history resound in an old street name, sometimes it is a shrill echo − at other times a faint murmur. Burrows Place and East Burrows Road fall into the latter category. Taken at face value, they are unremarkable road names and seem to have little meaning or relevance to us. However, in the eighteenth century, the land on which they now stand was grass-covered sand dunes, or burrows, over which Swansea's burgesses had common rights. In fact, as late as 1748 there was only one building on it and that was an inn serving the river ferry. Amazingly, Swansea would have to wait for over a century for a bridge to be built that would span the river in the town. By 1762, this traditional common land had been enclosed by the burgesses and became the focus for Swansea's tourism ambitions. A lawn and gravel walk was laid out at public expense on that portion of the Burrows nearest to the town and between the beach. The weather intervened in 1795, when the combination of a high spring tide and a following south-westerly inundated the area completely. The area was once more laid out as a pleasure ground and used as a parade ground by troops garrisoned in the castle. By 1786, the *Gloucester Journal* could assert that Swansea was 'the Brighton of Wales'. By the opening decades of the nineteenth century, the Burrows were definitely what was once called 'the most aristocratic part of Swansea'. By 1821, the Assembly Rooms had been built, as well as Cambrian Place (50 per cent of which still can be seen) and the terrace on Gloucester Place (1824). Prospect Place can also still be seen but much else, mostly designed by William Jernegan, has been demolished. To cap it all, the town hall was built there (now the Dylan Thomas Centre) in 1825, although the version we see now is a product of the Victorians.

Calvert Terrace was named after the pioneer photographer Calvert Richard Jones (1804-77). **Christina Street** was named after Jones's daughter and **Portia Street** after his second wife. **Veranda Street** was named after Jones's early home that stood in Singleton Park.

De La Beche Street was named after Sir Henry De La Beche (1796-1855) the distinguished geologist. In 1845, he presented a 'Report on the State of (Housing in) Bristol, Bath, Frome, Swansea, Merthyr Tydfil and Brecon' to the Health of Towns Commission.

Eaton Crescent in Uplands was named after Robert Eaton; a banker who owned a fine house called Bryn-Y-Môr on a knoll in the open country around Swansea in the 1820s. It still exists and is now known as the Stella Maris Ursuline convent. The horseshoe-shaped road that ran around it was called Eaton Crescent.

Fabian Way was named after a farmhouse belonging to a Daniel Fabian that used to exist where Inkerman Street in St Thomas is now. It was demolished in 1859 but you can still see what it looked like in a watercolour in Swansea Museum. Daniel Fabian held quite a lot of land in the area in 1764. There used to be a natural harbour called Fabian's Bay that stood where the Prince of Wales Dock now is, until it was partially filled in when the New Cut was created. If you wanted to get from, say, Briton Ferry to Swansea in the 1780s you had to use the northern edge of Fabian's Bay; however, high spring tides were periodically apt to wash this out. At some point before 1813, the route was moved to higher ground using the fields of Glanybad Farm for which Fabian's house was probably the farmhouse. Fabian's Bay began to be filled in from July 1879 in preparation for the creation of the Prince of Wales Dock, which was finished in 1881.

Fforestfach means 'little forest' and refers to a time when the area was heavily wooded.

Gendros was originally Cefn-Rhos. 'Cefn' meant 'back ridge' and 'rhos' meant 'moor or heath'. In 1735, this mutated in to Genrose thanks to an English clerk and by 1844 into Genrhos. By 1846 it was Gendros.

Graigola Road in Clydach comes from 'graig', meaning 'rock' in Welsh, and 'ola' could be a contraction of 'olaf', which means 'last'. Graigola colliery produced coal highly regarded for its steam-raising properties. Such coal was vital in an age of steamships, railway engines and any industrial concern that used a boiler. If you also allow for two to three fire grates in every house you can see the demand was enormous. By the early 1840s, over half a million tons of coal were being sent down the Swansea canal from the valleys for export. Swansea's local bituminous coal was soon in great demand worldwide and its position on the western rim of the South Wales coalfield meant that by the onset of the twentieth century it was the pre-eminent anthracite-exporting port in South Wales. Patent fuel, the mixing of coal dust and tar pitch to produce patent fuel blocks or briquettes made from coal began in Swansea in 1847. Such briquettes were roughly the size of a modern breezeblock and there were four to a cwt. They rolled along a conveyor belt and workers had to snatch them up and stack them for removal on a pallet. At the Graigola works they produced two basic types of patent fuel: one was the rectangular block shape and the other was a pellet roughly the size of a small bar of soap. They both left you filthy after a gruelling day packing them on the production line. Eight years later, Swansea was exporting 75 per cent of Britain's entire output, most of which went to France for commercial and domestic heating purposes. By the eve of the First World War, the amount being exported was only just short of 1 million tons a year. In 1915, the Graigola Merthyr Co. Ltd had its main factory at the King's Dock and contemporary posters boasted of an annual output of 7.5 million tons.

Inkerman Street, **Balaclava Street** and **Sebastopol Street** were all named after battles in the Crimean War (1854-56). **Delhi Street** in St Thomas was named after a battle in the Indian Mutiny (1857-59).

Mackworth Terrace in St Thomas originates with Sir Humphrey Mackworth (1657-1727), who was born in Shropshire. He married Mary Evans, an heiress to the Gnoll estate, in 1686 and by 1695 had established a smelting works at Melincryddan. Mackworth was nothing if not resourceful and quickly set about improving the performance of the various coal interests that came with his wife. He improved pit ventilation and built a tramway from his pits to the town quay. Mackworth was also responsible for introducing copper smelting and silver refining to Neath. In the nineteenth century, a Mackworth Arms Hotel stood in Wind Street but it was demolished to make way for a new central post office. It was also the start and finish point for all the stagecoaches going to and from Swansea. The name endures now as a street name in St Thomas and as the name of a housing development in High Street, **Mackworth Court**.

Miers Street appears to have to been named after the Miers family of Ynispenllwch, who settled in Wales from England in 1830. W.H. Jones, in his book *The History of the Port of Swansea* credits them with the introduction of the tinplate industry to the Neath and Swansea Valleys in the early nineteenth century.

Pentre Chwyth means 'windy village' and was probably inspired by the hillside location.

Pockett's Wharf in the Maritime Quarter owes its name not to clothing but to a family of Victorian shipowners. Walter Pockett (1794-1856) was a master mariner and merchant of the port of Swansea. He had five sons, all of whom worked in the business that had humble beginnings in the 1820s freighting fruit and vegetables between Swansea and Gloucester. By 1867, the wharfage area just above the entrance to South Dock was renamed Pockett's Wharf. The Pockett Steam Ship Company stayed in family ownership until 1890.

Robert Owen Gardens in Port Tennant is named after Robert Owen (1771-1858), arguably the most famous Welshman of his day and a utopian thinker. The son of a saddler and ironmonger from Newtown in Montgomeryshire, Owen became an industrialist who co-founded the New Lanark workers' community in Scotland during the late 1780s and 1790s. Owen's father-in-law was David Dale and between them they created a planned workers' community capable of housing 1,300 workers who were employed in Dale's vast textile mills. Owen, although now regarded as a visionary socialist, nevertheless exercised fairly draconian levels of social control in his workers' communities. He even went so far as to have employee patrols that would root out drunkenness among fellow workers. Owen's New Lanark had its own schools and the agenda was to produce good and humane people. Almost unique for his time, he deplored corporal punishment and unlike many another employer, would not employ children under the age of ten. Infants went to a nursery school and the older ones had to attend his secondary school for at least part of the day. He believed man was fundamentally good until corrupted by the world and its temptations. He also believed that environment formed character and to this end he went on to build New Lanark. By 1800, the New Lanark cotton mills were the largest cotton-spinning complex in Britain.

Taplow Terrace in Pentrechwyth is one of many street names that reflect the influence of the Grenfell family. It was named after the Buckinghamshire village on the Thames where the Grenfells had their family home and a rolling mill. **St Leger Crescent** was named not after the horse race but after Pascoe St Leger Grenfell (1798-1879). **Rifleman's Row** was also named in his honour because he raised a 200-strong local militia in 1859 called the 6th Glamorgan Rifle Corps and commanded it as Lieutenant Colonel. **Maesteg Park** in St Thomas was named after the Maesteg estate that existed on the Earl of Jersey's land above St Thomas. Riversdale William Grenfell (1807-71), an older brother of Pascoe St Leger, built Maesteg House in the 1840s and lived there until his death in 1879. There is also a **Maesteg Street**. Pascoe Du Pre Grenfell (1828-96), a son of Pascoe St Leger whose wife was Catherine Du Pre, gave his name to **Dupre Road** in St Thomas.

Worcester Place is where Admiral Nelson was given the Freedom of the Borough Town of Swansea in a ceremony on 2 August 1802. Thomas Morgan of Penderi, Llangyfelach, the Marquis of Worcester's steward, built himself a large townhouse in Swansea. As a compliment to the Marquis, he named his mansion Worcester House and the driveway became Worcester Place. It was destroyed by bombing in February 1941. The Marquis of Worcester cut the first sod of earth in a ceremony on 5 February 1852 on the Burrows, where the South Dock now stands. The ceremonial timber wheelbarrow and shovel used in that ceremony can still be seen in Swansea Museum.

About the author

Richard Porch has worked in the City of Swansea since 1986. He is a keen local historian who has spent many years exploring the streets of Swansea. This is his second book for Tempus Publishing.

The Maritime Quarter in 1975 (above) and in 2003 (below).

Other local titles published by Tempus

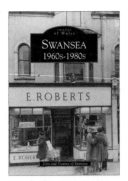

Swansea 1960s-1980s
CITY AND COUNTY OF SWANSEA

This impressive collection of photographs documents the changing face of Swansea over thirty years. During this important time, Swansea was transformed and this pictorial history records events such as the redevelopment of the Maritime Quarter and the city centre, including the construction of the Quadrant shopping centre in 1976. Anyone who knows Swansea, or has memories of the area as it once was, will find this book fascinating and informative.

0 7524 2456 4

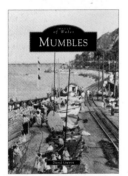

Mumbles
DAVID GWYNN

The famous Mumbles area of Swansea became a popular tourist destination after the first railway in the world to carry fare-paying passengers opened in 1804. It is now a thriving suburb, with pretty villages and attractive bays. Illustrated with over 200 old photographs and postcards, this book explores all aspects of life in the area. Images of working life, shops, schools and recreation create a vivid picture of times past.

0 7524 2858 6

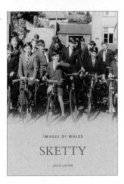

Sketty
DAVID GWYNN

This collection of more than 180 old photographs and postcards highlights some of the important events that have occurred in Sketty, including the Royal National Eisteddfod of Wales held at Singleton Park in 1907 and 1964, and recalls the everyday life of the local people who lived and worked in the area. *Sketty* will reawaken nostalgic memories for some, while offering a unique glimpse of this village's proud heritage for others.

0 7524 3380 6

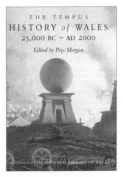

The Tempus History of Wales
PRYS MORGAN

Wales was at the heart of the Industrial Revolution, with towns like Merthyr Tydfil driving the engine of the British Empire. The cultural and social divide between modern, industrialised Wales and the traditional agricultural areas is explored within this comprehensive volume.

0 7524 1983 8

If you are interested in purchasing other books published by Tempus, or in case you have difficulty finding any Tempus books in your local bookshop, you can also place orders directly through our website

www.tempus-publishing.com